T0382174

THE SAYINGS OF JESUS
FROM OXYRHYNCHUS

THE
SAYINGS OF JESUS
FROM OXYRHYNCHUS

EDITED

WITH INTRODUCTION, CRITICAL
APPARATUS AND COMMENTARY

BY

HUGH G. EVELYN WHITE, M.A.

MEMBER OF THE NEW YORK METROPOLITAN MUSEUM
EXPEDITION IN EGYPT AND FORMERLY SCHOLAR OF
WADHAM COLLEGE, OXFORD

CAMBRIDGE
AT THE UNIVERSITY PRESS
1920

CAMBRIDGE
UNIVERSITY PRESS

University Printing House, Cambridge CB2 8BS, United Kingdom

Published in the United States of America by Cambridge University Press, New York

Cambridge University Press is part of the University of Cambridge.

It furthers the University's mission by disseminating knowledge in the pursuit of education, learning and research at the highest international levels of excellence.

www.cambridge.org
Information on this title: www.cambridge.org/9781107651708

© Cambridge University Press 1920

First published 1920
First paperback edition 2014

A catalogue record for this publication is available from the British Library

ISBN 978-1-107-65170-8 Paperback

Cambridge University Press has no responsibility for the persistence or accuracy of URLs for external or third-party internet websites referred to in this publication, and does not guarantee that any content on such websites is, or will remain, accurate or appropriate.

TO THE MEMORY OF

JEAN MASPERO

KILLED IN ACTION AT VAUQUOY IN THE ARGONNE

FEBRUARY 18, 1915

ERRATUM

P. 2, col. 2, . 21, and P. 48, col. 2, l. 8. *For* Litany of Sarapion, *read* Liturgy of Sarapion.

PREFACE

THE addition of one more item to the literature which has gathered round the famous Oxyrhynchus *Sayings* does not, in itself, need any apology; for large as that literature is, it has not solved all the problems which the papyrus fragments present, nor has it exhausted all the possibilities of text-reconstruction and interpretation. But inasmuch as I have no pass‑port admitting me to the realms of theology, my intrusion into what appears to be a theological province demands explanation. From one point of view, indeed, the *Sayings* seem to fall well within the demesne of theology, but from another to lie on the vague border land which parts theological from ancient literature in its broadest sense. I need hardly say that I prefer the latter. In this little study, therefore, I have regarded the fragments as remains of early Christian literature rather than as a theological document: the distinction, if fine, is real, and may serve to deliver me from the charge of exercising myself in great matters which are too high for me.

To multiply restorations of fragmentary texts is a process of doubtful benefit. Owing to accident my reconstructed text was drawn up before I had seen and weighed the restorations suggested by others; and though later study has led me considerably to modify my first draft, it has not prevented me from retaining certain supplements which take a new direction. That I have done so is due, I hope, neither to parental fondness for my own offspring nor to perverse love of novelty, but (if I may say so) to a feeling that the right track had not yet been found.

In the Introduction and Commentary I have tried not only to bring forward fresh considerations bearing upon the problems involved, but also to represent and consider the judgments of previous editors. This part of my work was begun in 1912 and continued during intervals of leisure in the following eighteen months. As a result I am conscious of a certain unevenness of treatment which recent revision has not, I fear, wholly eliminated.

For an editor to express obligations is often to accuse the guiltless of complicity. While, therefore, I cannot leave unspoken my very deep indebtedness to Professor J. F. Bethune Baker for much help and encouragement, I must add that I alone am responsible for my extravagances and my faults. With the late M. Jean Maspero I had the privilege of discussing many points relating to the *Sayings*, and it is to his memory therefore that I dedicate this little book.

I have to thank the Council of the Egypt Exploration Fund for permitting me to re-edit the fragments found by Professors Grenfell and Hunt under the auspices of that Society. I should also like to express my sincere gratitude to the Reader of the Cambridge University Press for the very great pains with which he has read my proofs, thereby saving me from a very formidable list of errors and imperfect references.

H. G. E. W.

CAMBRIDGE,
July 5, 1920.

CONTENTS

BIBLIOGRAPHY[1]

FRAGMENT I.

(Oxyrhynchus Papyri, no. 654.)

Bartlet, V. *The Oxyrhynchus Sayings of Jesus (Contemporary Review*, LXXXVII, 1905, pp. 116 ff. ; *Review of Theology and Philosophy*, I, pp. 11 ff.).

Batiffol, P. *Nouveaux Fragm. Évang. de Behnesa (Revue Biblique*, N.S. I, 1904, pp. 481 ff.).

Bruston, C. *Fragments d'un ancien Recueil de Paroles de Jésus*, Paris, 1905.

Deissmann, A. *Zur Text-Rekonstruktion der neusten Jesusworte aus Oxyrhynchos (Beilage zur Allgemeinen Zeitung*, July 18th, 1904, pp. 116 ff.).

Grenfell, B. P. and Hunt, A. S. *New Sayings of Jesus (Oxyrhynchus Papyri*, Pt IV, pp. 1 ff., no. 654)[2].

—— *New Sayings of Jesus and Fragments of a Lost Gospel*, Oxford, 1904.

Harnack, A. *Über einige Worte Jesu die nicht in den kanonischen Evangelien stehen (Sitz. d. k. preuss. Akad. d. Wissenschaften*, 1904, pp. 170 ff.).

Heinrici, G. *Die neuen Herrensprüchen (Theol. Stud. u. Krit.*, 1905, pp. 188 ff.).

—— *Die neuen Herrensprüchen (Theol. Literaturzeit.* XXIX, 1904, 428 ff.).

Hilgenfeld, A. *Neue Logia Jesu (Zeitschr. f. wissenschaftl. Theol.* N.S. XII, 1904, pp. 414 ff.).

Lake, K. *The New Sayings of Jesus and the Synoptic Problem (Hibbert Journal*, III, pp. 332 ff.).

---

[1] No attempt has been made to make this Bibliography exhaustive : it is select in the sense that it contains all the editions and studies which directly or indirectly have influenced the following pages.

[2] *Editio princeps.*

Lock, W. *The New Sayings of Jesus* (*Church Quarterly Rev.* LVIII, pp. 422 ff.).

—— *The Value of the "New Sayings of Jesus"* (*Interpreter*, I, pp. 30 ff.).

Swete, H. B. *The New Oxyrhynchus Sayings* (*Expository Times*, XV, pp. 488 ff.).

Taylor, C. *The Oxyrhynchus Sayings of Jesus*, Oxford, 1905.

—— *The Oxyrhynchus and other Agrapha* (*Journal of Theological Studies*, VII, 546 ff.).

Wessely, C. *Collections de prétendues Sentences de Jésus* (*Patrologia Orientalis*, IV, pp. 151 ff.).

Wilamowitz-Moellendorf, U. von. "*Oxyrhynchos Papyri* IV" (*Gött. Gel. Anzeiger*, 1904, pp. 659 ff.).

FRAGMENT II[1].

(Oxyrhynchus Papyri, no. 1.)

Badham, F. P. *The New Logia* (*Athenaeum*, Aug. 7th, 1897).

Bartlet, V. *The New Logia* (*Athenaeum*, July 24th, 1897).

Batiffol, P. *Les Logia du Papyrus de Behnesa* (*Revue Biblique*, VI, 1897, pp. 501 ff.).

Blass, F. (*Evang. Kirchenz.* 1897, pp. 498 ff.).

Bruston, C. *Les Paroles de Jésus*, Paris, 1898.

Cersoy, P. *Quelques Remarques sur les Logia de Behnesa* (*Revue Biblique*, VII, 1898, 415 ff.).

Clemen, C. *Neugefundene Jesusworte* (*Die Christliche Welt*, July 29th, 1897).

Davidson, T. (Review.) *International Journal of Ethics*, VIII, 106 ff.

Grenfell, B. P. and Hunt, A. S. ΛΟΓΙΑ ΙΗϹΟΥ, *Sayings of Our Lord from an early Greek Papyrus*[2], Oxford, 1897.

—— ΛΟΓΙΑ ΙΗϹΟΥ (*Oxyrhynchus Papyri*, Pt I, pp. 1 ff., no. 1).

Harnack, A. *Die jüngst entdeckten Sprüche Jesu*, Freiburg, 1897.

—— *The recently discovered Sayings of Jesus* (*Expositor*, 5th Series, VI, pp. 321 ff., 401 ff.)[3].

---

[1] For fuller bibliographies on this fragment, see Lock and Sanday, *Two Lectures on the Sayings of Jesus*, pp. 5 f.; Holtzmann in *Theol. Jahresb.* XVII, 115 ff., XVIII, 148 ff.

[2] *Editio princeps.*   [3] Translation of the foregoing.

Harris, J. R. *The Logia and the Gospels* (*Contemporary Review*, LXXII, pp. 341 ff.).

Heinrici, G. (Review.) (*Theöl. Litteraturzeitung*, XXII, 449 ff.).

Holtzmann, H. *Neue Sprüche Jesu* (*Prot. Monatsheft*, I, 385 ff.).

James, M. R. *The New Sayings of Christ* (*Contemporary Review*, LXXII, pp. 153 ff.).

Jülicher, A. Λόγια 'Ιησοῦ (*Gött. Gel. Anz.*, 1897, pp. 921 ff.).

Lock, W. and Sanday, W. *Two Lectures on the Sayings of Jesus*, Oxford, 1897.

Redpath, H. A. *The so-called Logia and their Relation to the Canonical Scriptures* (*Expositor*, 5th Series, VI, 224 ff.).

Reitzenstein, R. *Ein Zitat aus den Λόγια 'Ιησοῦ* (*Zeitschr. f. neutest. Wissenschaft u. Kunde*, VI, p. 203).

—— *Poimandres*, 239 ff., Leipzig, 1904.

Scholz, A. von. *Zu den Logia Jesu* (*Theol. Quartalschr.* 1900, pp. 1 ff.).

Swete, H. B. *The Oxyrhynchus Fragment* (*Expository Times*, Sept. 1897).

Taylor, C. *The Oxyrhynchus Logia and the Apocryphal Gospels*, Oxford, 1899.

Weiss, J. *Neue Logia* (*Theol. Rundschau*, I, 1898, pp. 227 ff.).

Wessely, C. (See Bibliography for Fragment I.)

Zahn, T. *Die jüngst gefundenen "Aussprüche Jesu"* (*Theol. Literaturblatt*, XVIII, 1897, pp. 417 ff., 425 ff.).

THE TEXT OF THE PAPYRI

(*Oxyrhynchus Papyri* 654)

οι τοιοι οι λογοι οι [
λησεν ΙΗΣ ο ζων κ[
και θωμα και ειπεν [
αν των λογων τουτ[
5 ου μη γευσηται‿[
μη παυσασθω ο ζη[
ευρη και οταν ευρ[
βηθεις βασιλευςη κ[
ησεται‿ λεγει ι[
10 οι ελκοντες ημας [
η βασιλεια εν ουρα[
τα πετεινα του ουρ[
τι ϋπο την γην εστ[
οι ϊχθυες της θαλα[
15 τες ϋμας και η βασ[
εντος ϋμων[..]ςτι [
γνω ταυτην ευρη[
εαυτους γνωσεσθαι [
   ϋμεις
εστε του πατρος του τ[
20 γνωσθε εαυτους εν[
και ϋμεις εστε η πτο[
ουκ αποκνησει ανθ[

ρων επερωτησε πα[
ρων περι του τοπου τη[
οτι
25 σετε πολλοι εσονται π[
οι εσχατοι πρωτοι και [
σιν λεγει ΙΗΣ‿[
θεν της οψεως σου και [
απο σου αποκαλυφησετ[
30 τιν κρυπτον ο ου φανε[
και τεθαμμενον ο ο[
[..]εταζουσιν αυτον οι [
[..]γουσιν πως νηστευ[
[.....]μεθα και πως [
35 [.....]αι τι παρατηρης[
[....]ν‿ λεγει ΙΗΣ [
[....]ειται μη ποιειτ[
[.....]ης αληθειας αν[
[........]ν α[ ]οκεκρ[
40 [.......]καρι [..] εστιν [
[..........]ω εστ[
[............]ιν[

    *   *   *

(Oxyrhynchus Papyri 1)

Verso ιλ

ΚΑΙ ΤΟΤΕ ΔΙΑΒΛΕΨΕΙC
ΕΚΒΑΛΕΙΝ ΤΟ ΚΑΡΦΟC
ΤΟ ΕΝ ΤΩ ΟΦΘΑΛΜΩ7
ΤΟΥ ΑΔΕΛΦΟΥ COY ΛΕΓΕΙ
5 ῙC ΕΑΝ ΜΗ ΝΗCΤΕΥCΗ
ΤΑΙ ΤΟΝ ΚΟCΜΟΝ ΟΥ ΜΗ
ΕΥΡΗΤΑΙ ΤΗΝ ΒΑCΙΛΕΙ
ΑΝ ΤΟΥ Θ̅Υ̅ ΚΑΙ ΕΑΝ ΜΗ
CΑΒΒΑΤΙCΗΤΕ ΤΟ CΑΒ7
10 ΒΑΤΟΝ ΟΥΚ ΟΨΕCΘΕ Τ̅Ο̅
Π̅Ρ̅Α̅ ΛΕΓΕΙ ῙC Ε[.]ΤΗΝ
ΕΝ ΜΕCΩ ΤΟΥ ΚΟCΜΟΥ
ΚΑΙ ΕΝ CΑΡΚΕΙ ΩΦΘΗΝ
ΑΥΤΟΙC ΚΑΙ ΕΥΡΟΝ ΠΑΝ
15 ΤΑC ΜΕΘΥΟΝΤΑC ΚΑΙ
ΟΥΔΕΝΑ ΕΥΡΟΝ ΔΕΙΨΩ̅
ΤΑ ΕΝ ΑΥΤΟΙC ΚΑΙ ΠΟ7
ΝΕΙ Η ΨΥΧΗ ΜΟΥ ΕΠΙ7
ΤΟΙC ΥΙΟΙC ΤΩΝ Α̅Ν̅Ω̅Ν̅
20 ΟΤΙ ΤΥΦΛΟΙ ΕΙCΙΝ ΤΗ ΚΑΡ
ΔΙΑ ΑΥΤΩ[.] ΚΑ̣Ι̣ .. ΒΛΕΠ
*　　*　　*　　*

Recto ε

[....]ε̣ι̣[..]ΗΝ ΠΤΩΧΙΑ̅
[...]ΕΙ[....]ΟΥ ΕΑΝ ΩCΙΝ
[....]Ε[...].. θ̣ΕΟΙ ΚΑΙ
[..]π̣ο̣.ε[..] ΕCΤΙΝ ΜΟΝΟC
5 [..]Γ̣Ω ΕΓΩ ΕΙΜΙ ΜΕΤ ΑΥ
Τ[..] ΕΓΕΙ [.]ΟΝ ΤΟΝ ΛΙΘ0̅
ΚΑΚΕΙ ΕΥΡΗCΕΙC ΜΕ
CΧΙCΟΝ ΤΟ Ξ̣ΥΛΟΝ ΚΑΓΩ
ΕΚΕΙ ΕΙΜΙ ΛΕΓΕΙ Ῑ̅C̅ ΟΥ
10 Κ ΕCΤΙΝ ΔΕΚΤΟC ΠΡΟ
ΦΗΤΗC ΕΝ ΤΗ Π̅Ρ̅Ι̅Δ̅Ι̅ ΑΥ
Τ[.]Υ ΟΥΔΕ ΙΑΤΡΟC ΠΟΙΕΙ
ΘΕΡΑΠΕΙΑC ΕΙC ΤΟΥC
ΓΕΙΝΩCΚΟΝΤΑC ΑΥΤΟ̅
15 ΛΕΓΕΙ Ῑ̅C̅ ΠΟΛΙC ΟΙΚΟΔΟ
ΜΗΜΕΝΗ ΕΠ ΑΚΡΟΝ
[.]ΡΟΥC ΥΨΗΛΟΥC ΚΑΙ ΕC
ΤΗΡΙΓΜΕΝΗ ΟΥΤΕ ΠΕ
[.]ΕΙΝ ΔΥΝΑΤΑΙ ΟΥΤΕ ΚΡΥ
20 [.]ΗΝΑΙ ΛΕΓΕΙ Ῑ̅C̅ ΑΚΟΥΕΙC
[.]ι̣C ΤΟ ε̣.. τ̣ΙΟΝ COY τ̣ο̣
*　　*　　*　　*

THE RESTORED TEXT[1]

οὗτοι οἱ λόγοι οἱ ζωοποιοὶ οὓς ἐλάλησεν Ἰησοῦς ὁ ζῶν
καὶ ὀφθεὶς τοῖς δέκα καὶ Θωμᾷ. καὶ εἶπεν αὐτοῖς· πᾶς
ὅστις ἂν τῶν λόγων τούτων ἀκούσῃ, θανάτου οὐ μὴ
γεύσηται.

α΄. λέγει Ἰησοῦς·
μὴ παυσάσθω ὁ ζητῶν τοῦ ζητεῖν ἕως ἂν εὕρῃ, καὶ
ὅταν εὕρῃ θαμβηθήσεται·
καὶ θαμβηθεὶς βασιλεύσει, καὶ βασιλεύσας ἀναπαήσεται.

β΄. λέγει Ἰούδας· τίνες ἄρα οἱ ἕλκοντες ἡμᾶς,
καὶ πότε ἐλεύσεται ἡ βασιλεία ἡ ἐν οὐρανοῖς οὖσα;
λέγει Ἰησοῦς·
τὰ πετεινὰ τοῦ οὐρανοῦ, καὶ τῶν θηρίων ὅτι ὑπὸ τὴν
γῆν ἐστιν ἢ ἐπὶ τῆς γῆς, καὶ οἱ ἰχθύες τῆς θαλάσσης—
οὗτοι οἱ ἕλκοντες ὑμᾶς.
καὶ ἡ βασιλεία τῶν οὐρανῶν ἐντὸς ὑμῶν ἐστι. καὶ
ὅστις ἂν ἑαυτὸν γνῷ ταύτην εὑρήσει· καὶ εὑρόντες αὐτὴν
ἑαυτοὺς γνώσεσθε ὅτι υἱοὶ καὶ κληρονόμοι ἐστε ὑμεῖς
τοῦ πατρὸς τοῦ παντοκράτορος· καὶ γνώσεσθε ἑαυτοὺς
ἐν θεῷ ὄντας καὶ θεὸν ἐν ὑμῖν. καὶ ὑμεῖς ἐστε ἡ πτόλις
θεοῦ.

γ΄. λέγει Ἰησοῦς·
οὐκ ἀποκνήσει ἄνθρωπος τὴν ὁδὸν εὑρὼν ἐπερωτῆσαι
πάντα...διαιρῶν περὶ τοῦ τόπου τῆς καθέδρας; εὑρήσετε

---

[1] The restorations are not here distinguished. The parallel clauses
are as far as possible indicated by the arrangement.

ὅτι πολλοὶ ἔσονται πρῶτοι ἔσχατοι, καὶ οἱ ἔσχατοι
πρῶτοι· καὶ ζωὴν κληρονομήσουσιν.

δ′. λέγει Ἰησοῦς·

πᾶν τὸ μὴ ἔμπροσθεν τῆς ὄψεώς σου,
καὶ τὸ κεκαλυμμένον ἀπό σου ἀποκαλυφθήσεταί σοι·
οὐ γάρ ἐστιν κρυπτὸν ὃ οὐ φανερὸν γενήσεται,
καὶ τεθαμμένον ὃ οὐκ ἐγερθήσεται.

ε′. ἐξετάζουσιν αὐτὸν οἱ μαθηταὶ αὐτοῦ καὶ λέγουσιν·
πῶς νηστεύσομεν, καὶ πῶς προσευξόμεθα, καὶ πῶς ἐλεημοσύνην ποιήσομεν, καὶ τί παρατηρήσομεν τῶν παραδοθέντων;

λέγει Ἰησοῦς·
οὐκ ἔσεσθε ὡς οἱ ὑποκριταί· μὴ ποιεῖτε ταῦτα φανε-
ρῶς·
ἀλλὰ τῆς ἀληθείας ἀντέχεσθε, καὶ ἡ δικαιοσύνη ὑμῶν
ἀποκεκρυμμένη ἔστω.

λέγω γάρ·
μακάριός ἐστιν ὁ ταῦτα ποιῶν ἐν κρυπτῷ,
ὅτι ἐν φανερῷ ἔσται ὁ μισθὸς αὐτοῦ παρὰ τῷ πατρὶ
ὅς ἐστιν ἐν τοῖς οὐρανοῖς.

*   *   *

ϛ′. λέγει Ἰησοῦς·
ἔκβαλλε πρῶτον τὴν δοκὸν ἐκ τοῦ ὀφθαλμοῦ σου,
καὶ τότε διαβλέψεις ἐκβαλεῖν τὸ κάρφος τὸ ἐν τῷ
ὀφθαλμῷ τοῦ ἀδελφοῦ σου.

ζ′. λέγει Ἰησοῦς·
ἐὰν μὴ νηστεύσητε τὸν κόσμον, οὐ μὴ εὕρητε τὴν
βασιλείαν τοῦ θεοῦ·
καὶ ἐὰν μὴ σαββατίσητε τὸ σάββατον, οὐκ ὄψεσθε
τὸν πατέρα.

η΄. λέγει Ἰησοῦς·
ἔστην ἐν μέσῳ τοῦ κόσμου, καὶ ἐν σαρκὶ ὤφθην αὐτοῖς·
καὶ εὗρον πάντας μεθύοντας, καὶ οὐδένα εὗρον διψῶντα
    ἐν αὐτοῖς·
καὶ πονεῖ ἡ ψυχή μου ἐπὶ τοῖς υἱοῖς τῶν ἀνθρώπων,
ὅτι τυφλοί εἰσιν τῇ καρδίᾳ αὐτῶν,
καὶ οὐ βλέπουσι τῇ διανοίᾳ αὐτῶν.

θ΄. λέγει Ἰησοῦς·
. . . ειν τὴν πτωχείαν . . .

ι΄. λέγει Ἰησοῦς·
ὅπου ἐὰν ὦσιν β΄, οὔκ εἰσιν ἄθεοι·
καὶ ὅπου εἷς ἐστιν μόνος, λέγω ἐγώ εἰμι μετ᾽ αὐτοῦ.
ἔγειρον τὸν λίθον, κἀκεῖ εὑρήσεις με,
σχίσον τὸ ξύλον, κἀγὼ ἐκεῖ εἰμι.

ια΄. λέγει Ἰησοῦς·
οὐκ ἔστιν δεκτὸς προφήτης ἐν τῇ πατρίδι αὐτοῦ,
οὐδὲ ἰατρὸς ποιεῖ θεραπείας εἰς τοὺς γινώσκοντας
    αὐτόν.

ιβ΄. λέγει Ἰησοῦς·
πόλις ᾠκοδομημένη ἐπ᾽ ἄκρον ὄρους ὑψηλοῦ καὶ
    ἐστηριγμένη
οὔτε πεσεῖν δύναται οὔτε κρυβῆναι.

ιγ΄. λέγει Ἰησοῦς·
ἀκούεις εἰς τὸ ἓν ὠτίον σου,
τὸ δὲ ἕτερον συνέκλεισας.

INTRODUCTION

§ I. THE PAPYRI.

In 1897 Messrs B. P. Grenfell and A. S. Hunt, while
excavating on behalf of the Graeco-Roman Branch of the
Egypt Exploration Fund, recovered from one of the rubbish-
mounds of the city of Oxyrhynchus a leaf of a papyrus book
containing eight (or, as some think, seven) Sayings of Jesus[1].
This fragment, which measures 15 cm. by 9 cm. in its actual
state, is a leaf from a codex and is inscribed on both sides.
The lower edge of the leaf is broken leaving no indication
to show how much has been lost. While the discoverers
think that as many as five or even ten lines may have been
lost, on the ground that the page of an early codex such as
this would resemble the high, narrow column of a papyrus
roll[2], later editors fascinated by the temptation of combining
Sayings VIII and IX [Logia III and IV], claim that what has
been lost is not great in amount, and that the lacuna between
the texts of the *recto* and *verso* can be bridged by restoration:
I have preferred to follow the expert authority of Grenfell
and Hunt. The upper edge of the leaf has not suffered
severely, and the right-hand side is also intact, but the left
side is very ragged, though fragments of the original edge
seem to be preserved here and there[3]. There is an ample

---

[1] Published by the discoverers under the title Λόγια Ἰησοῦ, Sayings
of our Lord (Frowde, 1897), and in *Oxyrhynchus Papyri*, Vol. I, No. 1.
Since the discovery of *Ox. Pap.* 654 the term Logia as applied to these
Sayings has been proved to be mistaken: it is abandoned in this edition.
The original is now in the Semitic Library, Harvard.

[2] *Ox. Pap.* I, p. 1.

[3] So far as I can judge from the facsimile in the *editio princeps*.

upper margin, while the left and right margins are decidedly narrower: a strip of papyrus has been gummed along the left edge of the *recto*. A few holes in the area of the text do not in themselves constitute formidable lacunae; but while the *verso* is tolerably legible throughout, the writing on the left side of the *recto* is rubbed or faded and far less distinct.

The discoverers concluded that the *verso* (which bears the numeral[1] ιΔ, written by a later hand, at the top right-hand corner of the text) came uppermost in the book, "since it was usual to foliate the right-hand pages of a book." A page from a codex of Sophocles[2] also shows the *verso* uppermost: the *verso* indeed must necessarily come uppermost as often as the *recto* where a codex consists in gatherings of sheets once folded. Grenfell and Hunt advance another reason for their conclusion which is surely decisive. The scribe has filled out the ends of his short lines on the *verso* with the character ⁊: this device is intended to make the outer edge of the text even throughout, just as mediaeval cutters of inscriptions, scribes, and printers fill out short lines with pieces of conventional ornament. On the *recto* no such device is used, surely because this side was undermost and the ends of the lines being next the inner edge (and so less conspicuous) did not need such filling out.

This conclusion has been disputed by Batiffol[3], who argues that it was usual to number the last page of each quire in a codex and that the papyrus is, therefore, the last leaf of the eleventh quire of a codex, the *recto* lying uppermost. He thinks that the ragged left edge of the *verso* has reached its present shredded state because it was the outer edge and so exposed to wear, and that the slip of papyrus gummed along the left border of the *recto* (which the discoverers explain as

---

[1] Wessely (*P. O.* IV, p. 153) treats the ιΔ not as a numeral, but as a correction.

[2] *Ox. Pap.* I, no. 22 (pp. 47 sqq.).

[3] *Revue Biblique*, 1897, p. 502.

intended to strengthen the outer margin) is simply a trace
of the juxtaposition of another leaf. This last point can
only be decided by experts after examination of the original;
but it may be remarked here that the ragged state of the
left edge of the *verso* is very likely due to the tearing out of
the leaf, and that Batiffol overlooks the fact that in any
quire there would be as many *versos* uppermost as *rectos*.
There is, then, no good reason for doubting the discoverers'
conclusion.

In general the ·papyri found in the rubbish-mounds of
Oxyrhynchus date from the first to the eighth century, but
the mound which yielded the fragment under consideration
contained a great number of papyri of the first three centuries
of the Christian era[1], and the Sayings were found in immediate association with documents of the second and third
centuries. The hand is typical of the Roman period and
indicates 300 A.D. as the latest date to which the MS. can
be assigned, while the Biblical contractions, ΙC̄, Θ̄C, Π̄Ρ, ᾹΝΟC̄
together with the codex-form as opposed to the roll-form
make an earlier date than 100 A.D. impossible and 150 A.D.
unlikely as a *terminus ante quem*. The discoverers, con-
sidering that the type of uncial here used is decidedly earlier
than that in use immediately before 300 A.D., conclude that
the probable date of their papyrus is not much later than
200 A.D.[2]

In addition to the contractions already mentioned, final Ν
is sometimes represented by a stroke over the preceding
vowel, and in the fifth so-called Logion (Saying X) the word
δύο was written in numeral form β'. Marks of punctuation
are wholly absent, but a sign ⁊—as we have already seen—
is used for filling in blank spaces at the end of lines.
Some eccentricities in orthography, such as are common in
Egyptian Greek, occur: *e.g.* ΑΙ for Є and ЄΙ for Ι: in ll. 36 and

---

[1] *Eg. Expl. Fund Arch. Rep.* 1896–7, p. 6: Λόγια Ἰησοῦ, p. 5.
[2] See Λόγια Ἰησοῦ, p. 6.

38 mistakes are found, but the second of these has been corrected.

Each Saying is introduced by the formula λέγει Ἰησοῦς[1], and the regular use of this together with the codex form, the use of practically no abbreviations other than Biblical, prove the papyrus to be a fragment of a literary work and not a series of notes or jottings for temporary use.

In 1903 the same two scholars resumed work at Oxyrhynchus and found a second papyrus containing five further Sayings of Jesus preceded by a Prologue[2]. The new fragment is part of a roll, ·244 m. high by ·078 m. wide, and, as it stands, is easily legible throughout. The entire right-hand side of the column has been lost, so that only one half of each of the 42 lines it contains has been preserved. Moreover, after l. 31 the beginnings of the lines also have been destroyed, the lacunae increasing as we descend until in l. 42 only two characters remain. These Sayings are written upon the *verso* of the roll, the *recto* being occupied by a land-survey list in a cursive hand which belongs to the end of the second or early part of the third century A.D. The hand of the *verso* is "an upright, informal uncial of medium size," not so fine as that of the fragment found in 1897, but clear and well-formed, which the discoverers assign to the middle or end of the third century. A date later than 300 A.D. is regarded as most unlikely by them[3]. The new papyrus (hereafter referred to as 654) is therefore nearly contemporary with the "Logia-fragment," which is assigned to an earlier decade in the third century.

[1] For a discussion of this formula see below, § 9.
[2] Published by the discoverers in *Oxyrhynchus Papyri*, Vol. IV, as no. 654, and, with less detail, in the Egypt Exploration Fund's *New Sayings of Jesus and Fragment of a lost Gospel* (Frowde, London and New York, 1904). I have borrowed the term Prologue in preference to Introduction from Dr Swete, as the latter seems to misrepresent the character of the opening five lines.
[3] For this section see *Ox. Pap.* IV, pp. 1 ff.

The only abbreviation which occurs is the normal ι͞η͞ς¹.
The scribe places diaeresis over initial ï and ÿ, but has
employed no punctuation marks. Though the words are
sometimes separated, this is by no means generally or
systematically done. In ll. 20, 25, words have been omitted
but subsequently supplied above the line. In l. 1 there is
obviously an uncorrected mistake, as also in l. 20; and in
ll. 18, 23 and 31 are eccentricities, ΑΙ for ε, ε for ΑΙ, such as
are common in Egyptian papyri and ostraka. The end of
each Saying² is marked by the *coronis* ⲭ, and is marked off
from the following Saying by a *paragraphus*, a horizontal
stroke drawn from the margin between the two Sayings.

The use of these signs together with the uncial script, the
general absence of abbreviations, the systematic use of the
formula λέγει Ἰησοῦς before each Saying, and above all the
presence of a *Prologue*, prove that **654**, like **1**, is a fragment
of a literary work³.

§ 2. THE OXYRHYNCHUS COLLECTION.

The results of the preceding section may be summed up
as follows: (1) both **1** and **654** are fragments from literary
works, (2) both were written during the third century and
probably in its earlier half, though **1** is considered by the discoverers to be the earlier by a few decades.

Did these two fragments belong to one Collection? Of
course they do not come from the same MS., since **1** is from
a codex and **654** from a roll; but they may represent two

¹ But others may well have occurred in the missing portion of the
papyrus.
² In l. 27 the coronis is placed after the formula λέγει Ἰησοῦς obviously by accident, and in l. 36 at the end of the series of questions put
by the disciples.
³ The discoverers (*Ox. Pap.* IV, p. 1) point out that there is nothing
at all uncommon in the use of the back of an ephemeral document for a
literary text.

copies of the same document. Now **1** is numbered ιᴀ and
is therefore the eleventh leaf of a codex: it contains eight
Sayings. If we allow for the occasional occurrence of longer
Sayings, such as the second and fifth in **654**, we may conclude that on an average each leaf of the codex to which
1 belonged contained five Sayings: more than fifty Sayings
must therefore have preceded **1**, which, moreover, need not
have been the last page in the codex, and the Collection which
it represents must have been a large one. The same may
be said of the Collection of which **654** is a fragment, for the
papyrus begins with a formal Prologue which would be unsuitable to anything but a work of some length; and the
text is written on the back of a document which is likely to
have been a long one[1]. When we recall further that both
fragments are of one provenance and are approximately of
one date, we have a good *prima facie* case for treating them
as parts of one and the same Collection. Internal evidence
bears this out. (1) The use of λέγει Ἰησοῦς absolutely, as a
formula to introduce Sayings is unique—though this argument is not very forcible since the Oxyrhynchus fragments are
the only extant remains of any formal collection of Sayings
of Jesus. (2) The peculiar relation of both to the canonical
Gospels is the same in the character of their divergencies and
resemblances alike[2]. (3) Both show distinct traces of the
influence of Hebrew literature[3]. (4) The general level of
thought, the doctrinal development, and the colouring is
equal in both fragments. And in pure style there is the same
similarity: if the parallelistic form of the Sayings in **1** is not
as uniformly present in **654**, this means no more than that
at some points in his source the compiler of the Collection
found much, and at others little parallelistic matter; and as
a matter of fact at least one, if not two, Sayings in **654** are

---

[1] See *Ox. Pap.* IV, pp. 2, 10.
[2] See § 4 (pp. xxxiv ff.), where this subject is discussed in detail.
[3] Pp. lxiii ff.

cast in this shape (Sayings IV and V). Similarly the presence
of a context in Saying V (and probably in Saying II), and the
greater length of two of the Sayings in 654 are due to purely
accidental causes. Here the compiler of the Collection might
find short epigrammatic utterances, here longer Sayings which
needed something of a context to bring out their meaning,
—and would wish to include both alike in his "Treasury."

All our evidence then, so far as it goes, distinctly favours
the supposition that 654 is the first part of a literary Collection of Sayings, to which 1 also belonged.

§ 3. COLLECTIONS OF SAYINGS IN GENERAL.

Is the Oxyrhynchus Collection unique in Christian literature, or is it but one example of a numerous class? The
answer to this question must obviously determine the stand-
point from which we regard this document. And first we
must remember that Collections of noteworthy Sayings are
by no means unknown in literature generally. The Jews
preserved the Sayings of their famous doctors in the Talmud
and later in the Collection known as *Pirke Aboth*; and since
Jewish colonies were to be found in many parts of Egypt, and
Jewish influence was necessarily strong in the early Christian
period, it is not impossible that the Oxyrhynchus Collection
was formed, directly or indirectly, after a Hebraic model[1].
But it is not necessary to assume this. The Egyptian also
was naturally inclined to form Collections of Sayings, recording in aphoristic form the virtues and teaching of famous
men; and the *Apophthegmata Patrum*[2] has come down to us
as a remarkable fruit of this tendency, while the *Precepts of
Ptah-hotep*[3] is partly preserved to us as a somewhat similar

[1] Lock and Sanday, *Two Lectures*, p. 48.
[2] For a Greek text of the alphabetic recension see Migne's *Patrologia
Graeca*, LXV, cols. 71 ff. On the origin and date of this and other
recensions see Butler, *Laus. Hist. of Palladius*, I, pp. 208 ff.
[3] See Budge, *Literature of the Egyptians*, pp. 224 ff. To the same
general class belong the *Maxims of Ani* (see *op. cit.* pp. 228 ff.).

monument from the Dynastic Period. We need not therefore
go outside Egypt to find the origin of such literature.
The discoverers have suggested that the Oxyrhynchus Collection may well have been but one of many such works and
cite the *Logia* of Matthew and the *Logia Kyriaka* on which
Papias commented as other examples of Collections of
Sayings, though they regard the possibility of a connection
between either of these and the document found by them as
entirely remote. What, then, was the nature of the two works
referred to, and were they in their general structure and scope
similar to the Oxyrhynchus Collection? In this connection
Dr Lock[1] has remarked that in the first and second centuries
the term λόγια or τὰ λόγια with Θεοῦ, or τοῦ Κυρίου, or Κυριακά
added, generally seems to mean either the Old Testament
or the whole Gospel message, while the combination λόγια
Ἰησοῦ is never found: accordingly he suggested (in 1897)
that the true title of the Oxyrhynchus Collection was λόγοι
Ἰησοῦ[2]—a brilliant conjecture which was confirmed by the
discovery of **654**. But Papias[3] in his notice of Mark's Gospel
and Matthew's *Logia* seems to equate λόγοι and λόγια, though
the latter term, no doubt, has the fuller meaning "*inspired*
Sayings." I therefore take λόγια and λόγοι alike to mean
"Sayings." The passage is very important for an investiga-
tion of the nature of the *Logia* of Matthew and the *Logia
Kyriaka*: it may here be quoted in full. καὶ τοῦθ᾽ ὁ πρεσ-
βύτερος ἔλεγεν· Μάρκος μὲν ἑρμηνευτὴς Πέτρου γενόμενος ὅσα
ἐμνημόνευσεν ἀκριβῶς ἔγραψεν, οὐ μέντοι τάξει τὰ ὑπὸ τοῦ
Χριστοῦ ἢ λεχθέντα ἢ πραχθέντα· οὔτε γὰρ ἤκουσεν τοῦ
Κυρίου, οὔτε παρηκολούθησεν αὐτῷ, ὕστερον δέ, ὡς ἔφην, Πέτρῳ·
ὃς πρὸς τὰς χρείας ἐποιεῖτο τὰς διδασκαλίας, ἀλλ᾽ οὐχ ὥσπερ
σύνταξιν τῶν κυριακῶν ποιούμενος λόγων. ὥστε οὐδὲν ἥμαρτεν
Μάρκος, οὕτως ἔνια γράψας ὡς ἀπεμνημόνευσεν. ἑνὸς γὰρ ἐποιή-

[1] *Two Lectures*, p. 16.
[2] For λόγος = 'Saying' (in our sense) cp. *Matth.* xv 12.
[3] *ap.* Eusebius *H. E.* III, 39. 15, 16.

σατο πρόνοιαν, τοῦ μηδὲν ὧν ἤκουσεν παραλιπεῖν ἢ ψεύσασθαί
τι ἐν αὐτοῖς. ταῦτα μὲν οὖν ἱστόρηται τῷ Παπίᾳ περὶ τοῦ
Μάρκου. περὶ δὲ τοῦ Ματθαίου ταῦτ᾽ εἴρηται· Ματθαῖος μὲν οὖν
Ἑβραΐδι διαλέκτῳ τὰ λόγια συνετάξατο, ἡρμήνευσεν δ᾽ αὐτὰ ὡς
ἠδύνατο ἕκαστος.

I am reminded that the view that Papias' work dealt not
with Sayings of our Lord, but with Messianic prophecies—
which, of course, occupy a larger place in *Matthew* than in
any other Gospel—is now gaining considerable ground. It
is impossible to enter here upon a discussion of the nature
of Papias' work ; nor am I qualified to do so. But surely the
evidence before us goes to show that unrecorded Sayings,
parables and acts of our Lord were the materials Papias collected and dealt with. Cp. the words of Eusebius where
after recording the miraculous deliverance of Justus Barsabas
he adds : (§ 11) καὶ ἄλλα δὲ ὁ αὐτὸς ὡσὰν ἐκ παραδόσεως ἀγράφου εἰς αὐτὸν ἤκοντα παρατέθειται, ξένας τέ τινας παραβολὰς τοῦ
σωτῆρος καὶ διδασκαλίας αὐτοῦ καί τινα ἄλλα μυθικώτερα. It is
difficult to see how such material and traditions, such as the
death of St John the Divine, the incident of the woman
" accused of many sins before the Lord " would be fitted into
a disquisition on Messianic prophecies. Again, Papias as
reported by Eusebius (III, 39. 4) tells us that : τοὺς τῶν πρεσβυτέρων ἀνέκρινον λόγους, τί Ἀνδρέας ἢ τί Πέτρος εἶπεν ἢ τί
Φίλιππος ἢ τί Θωμᾶς ἢ Ἰάκωβος ἢ τί Ἰωάννης ἢ Ματθαῖος ἤ τις
ἕτερος τῶν τοῦ κυρίου μαθητῶν. It is doubtful if he would in
this way obtain much to enrich a work on Messianic prophecies ; but he would be likely to hear of many unrecorded
Sayings, Discourses and the like. On the one hand Papias
seems to disparage a side of Mark's work : it was composed for special needs, and the Sayings or discourses of the
Lord were somewhat loosely and disjointedly set down (οὐχ
ὥσπερ σύνταξιν τῶν κυριακῶν ποιούμενος λόγων) ; on the other,
he appears to find Matthew's work superior in this respect,
though some difficulty in the rendering or interpretation of

it arose from the use of the "Hebrew dialect" (Ματθαῖος μὲν οὖν Ἑβραΐδι διαλέκτῳ τὰ λόγια συνετάξατο [v.l. συνεγράψατο], ἡρμήνευσεν δ᾽ αὐτὰ ὡς ἠδύνατο ἕκαστος). When we recall that Papias is commenting on *Sayings* of the Lord we can hardly doubt the reason for this comparison between the two works as συντάξεις λόγων : he is choosing the *Logia* of Matthew as the subject of his Commentary[1] and explaining why he preferred this work to Mark's Gospel. The remark ἡρμήνευσεν δ᾽ αὐτὰ ὡς ἠδύνατο ἕκαστος is accounted for by the fact that Papias proposes to give ἑρμηνεῖαι of his own : he implies, of course, that this interpretation had hitherto been ill done and that his own would be authoritative. The *Logia* of Matthew and the λόγια Κυριακά on which Papias commented are therefore, on this view, one and the same.

This identification is also made by Kirsopp Lake on different grounds[2]. It is known that the Commentary of Papias was in five books, and Sir John Hawkins has pointed out[3] that the First Gospel shows signs of an underlying document divided into five "pereḳs" or chapters, the ends of which appear in *Matth*. vii 28, xi 1, xiii 53, xix 1, xxvi 1— roughly in the form καὶ ἐγένετο ὅτε ἐτέλεσεν Ἰησοῦς τοὺς λόγους τούτους.... Presumably the underlying document is the *Logia* of Matthew, a fact which would account for the otherwise difficult ascription of the First Gospel to Matthew.

The *Logia* of Matthew and the *Logia Kyriaka* resolve themselves on this argument into Q, the non-Marcan source of the First and Third Gospels. Now though there may be some disagreement as to the exact shape and

---

[1] Papias clearly worked on the basis of an accepted document and grouped his real material round those passages which it seemed to supplement and explain. Compare Papias' own words συγκατατάξαι ταῖς ἑρμηνείαις, and the account of Eusebius (*H. E.* III, 39. 11) καὶ ἄλλα δὲ ὁ αὐτὸς ὡσὰν ἐκ παραδόσεως ἀγράφου...π α ρ α τ έ θ ε ι τ α ι, ξένας τέ τινας παραβολὰς τοῦ σωτῆρος κ.τ.λ.

[2] *Hibbert Journal*, III, pp. 337–8.

[3] *Horae Synopticae*, 131–5.

details of Q, its general form and nature is clear : it con-
sisted in discourses and parables, with some short Sayings
and, apparently, brief narrative connections. This is a document totally different from the Oxyrhynchus Collection
which is a series of short, independent Sayings without any
connections either of narrative or (apparently) of subject.
Professor Lake[1] has indeed suggested a connection between
the Oxyrhynchus Sayings and Q by an analysis of *Luke* i 1–4.
He points out that in the clause ἵνα ἐπιγνῷς περὶ ὧν κατηχήθης λόγων τὴν ἀσφάλειαν, the word κατηχήθης has a technical sound, and asks: can these λόγοι be a series of Sayings
used for the instruction of converts which Luke is providing
with a historical framework ? If so, οἱ λόγοι is equivalent to
Q and was used by Luke directly, while the First Gospel is
based upon a recension known as λόγια—the Matthaean
Logia of Papias. But there is no need to suppose Luke
means more by λόγοι here than "matters," "subjects"—even
if κατηχήθης be given its full technical sense ; and in any
case the Q of Luke like the Q of Matthew (supposing them
to have used different recensions) must still have been totally
unlike the Oxyrhynchus Collection.

The *Logia* of Matthew, then, together with its equivalents
and semi-equivalents cannot—so far as our evidence enables
us to judge—have been in any sense analogous to the
Oxyrhynchus Sayings.

Is it possible to discern behind the Synoptic Gospels and
behind, or independent of, Q a primitive Collection of
Sayings which is comparable to that of Oxyrhynchus ? The
theory that in the earliest days of Christianity there existed
a Collection of Sayings was enthusiastically championed by
Dr Rendel Harris[2] after the publication of I, was accepted
and advanced a stage by Professor Lake[3] after the appear-

---

[1] *Hibbert Journal*, III, p. 337.
[2] *Contemp. Rev.* 1897, p. 346.
[3] *Hibbert Journal*, III, pp. 332 ff.

ance of **654**, and has even found a follower in Dr Harnack[1] (who identifies this document with Q). Harris pointed out that *agrapha* are quoted by St Paul[2], Clement of Rome, and Polycarp with an introductory formula which varies but little, wherever used, and considered that the constancy with which this distinctive formula is used indicates that it is borrowed from a Collection of Sayings. The passages in question are as follows:

(1) *Acts* xx 35 δεῖ...μνημονεύειν τῶν λόγων τοῦ κυρίου Ἰησοῦ ὅτι αὐτὸς εἶπεν· κ.τ.λ.

(2) i *Clem. Rom.* XIII μάλιστα μεμνημένοι τῶν λόγων τοῦ κυρίου Ἰησοῦ οὓς ἐλάλησεν διδάσκων ἐπιείκειαν καὶ μακροθυμίαν· οὕτως γὰρ εἶπεν κ.τ.λ.

(3) *Id.* XLVI μνήσθητε τῶν λόγων Ἰησοῦ τοῦ κυρίου ἡμῶν· εἶπε γάρ· κ.τ.λ.

(4) Polycarp, *ad Philipp.* II μνημονεύοντες δὲ ὧν εἶπεν ὁ κύριος διδάσκων, κ.τ.λ.

Since, however, Polycarp appears to have borrowed both formula and *agraphon* from Clement, St Paul and Clement of Rome stand alone as authorities for this formula. Professor Lake[3] claims that in the Prologue of **654** we have another example of this citation-formula and one which by its position at the head of a series of Sayings vindicates Harris' theory in the most striking way. And indeed at first sight the words οὗτοι οἱ λόγοι...οὓς ἐλάλησεν Ἰησοῦς...καὶ εἶπεν seem to lie very near to the introduction used by St Paul and Clement. Closer examination does not confirm this. In St Paul and in Clement ὅτι εἶπεν (or its equivalent) is always epexegetic of οἱ λόγοι, whereas the author of the Prologue makes οἱ λόγοι cover the whole Collection, and uses καὶ εἶπεν to introduce a casual citation

[1] *The Sayings of Jesus* (E.T.), pp. 188-9.
[2] St Paul has another logion (but without formula) in I Cor. xiii 2 κἂν ἔχω πᾶσαν τὴν πίστιν ὥστε ὄρη μεθιστάνειν (cf. *Matth.* xxi 21).
[3] *Hibbert Journal*, III, 334.

intended to clinch a point which he is driving home. The Prologue of **654** cannot therefore be held to support Dr Harris' theory.

The main position moreover is open to attack from more than one side. Clement's earlier citation does not seem to be a *Logos* at all (in the technical sense) for the writer clearly indicates that it is taken from a discourse on ἐπιείκεια and μακροθυμία: and there is nothing to show that the same may not be true of the remaining examples. Again, the " formula " is by no means necessarily borrowed from a Collection: in itself it is a natural hieratic form such as would, when once established, come in very general use[1]. But above all we find the " formula " or very close approximations to it in the Gospels and elsewhere in contexts which do not allow us to regard it as a loan from a Collection of our Lord's Sayings.

(1) *Luke* xxii 61 καὶ ὑπεμνήσθη ὁ Πέτρος τοῦ ῥήματος τοῦ κυρίου ὡς εἶπεν αὐτῷ ὅτι....

(2) *Id.* xxiv 6 μνήσθητε ὡς ἐλάλησεν ὑμῖν...λέγων....

(3) *Ib.* 44 οὗτοι οἱ λόγοι μου οὓς ἐλάλησα πρὸς ὑμᾶς ὅτι....

(4) *Acts* xi 16 ὑπεμνήσθην δὲ τοῦ ῥήματος κυρίου ὡς ἔλεγεν· Ἰωάννης μὲν ἐβάπτισεν ὕδατι....

(5) *John* xv 20 μνημονεύετε τοῦ λόγου οὗ ἐγὼ εἶπον ὑμῖν.

(6) *Id.* xvi 4 ἀλλὰ ταῦτα λελάληκα ἵνα...μνημονεύητε αὐτῶν ὅτι ἐγὼ εἶπον ὑμῖν.

(7) *Jude* 17 ὑμεῖς δέ, ἀγαπητοί, μνήσθητε τῶν ῥημάτων τῶν προειρημένων ὑπὸ τῶν ἀποστόλων...ὅτι ἔλεγον ὑμῖν....

(8) *Clem. Hom.* XIX 20 μεμνήμεθα τοῦ κυρίου ἡμῶν καὶ διδασκάλου ὡς ἐντελλόμενος εἶπεν ἡμῖν....

(9) Epiphanius, *Haer.* LXIV 5 μνημονεύετε τῶν λόγων κυρίου ὅτι αὐτὸς εἶπεν....

---

[1] Just as "You will remember how our Lord says " is a stock pulpit-phrase at the present day.

Of these passages (8) alone introduces an *agraphon* (pre-viously overlooked in this connection), and if we are to maintain that the "formula" is still derived from a Collec-tion, we must be equally prepared to maintain the proba-bility that our Lord (as in 3, 5 and 6) and the angels at the Sepulchre (as in 2) would be represented as quoting a citation-formula from a Collection; we must explain why Luke uses it in (1) as part of his ordinary narrative, and why Peter in (4) uses it to preface a Saying which he remembers to have heard himself from Jesus. Are we, lastly, to infer from (7) that there was also a Collection of Sayings of the Apostles introduced by the same formula? The example quoted from Epiphanius gives the key to the whole matter. Formula and citation are there borrowed from *Acts* xx 35, and we have already seen that Polycarp borrows the formula (with an *agraphon*) from Clement of Rome. The form of citation is solemn and impressive and, as we have said, once it had taken root, it would spread widely. It is by no means unlikely that Luke—who has no less than five examples—was the first to make it current coin; but in its origin it seems to be merely a natural homiletic expression. May it not be that Luke learnt it from St Paul himself, not at Ephesus alone, but in the general course of his preaching, absorbed it into his own literary stock, and so passed it on to other writers? We conclude, then, that the citation-formula of Paul and Clement cannot be held to be evidence for the existence of a Collection of Sayings—much less of a Collection analogous in type to the Oxyrhynchus Sayings of Jesus.

Lastly, can we discern such a primitive Collection in the two sources of the Synoptic Gospels, Mark and Q? The second of these contained a number of Sayings which are short, epigrammatic, and often parallelistic in form: *Luke* vi 27 ff. and *Matth.* v 13 ff. may be mentioned as special repositories of such Sayings. These *logoi* are exactly what

we should expect to find in a primitive Collection. In many
cases they are quite arbitrarily introduced without context,
and in others owe their grouping to an editor's striving
after σύνταξις. The probability that these isolated *logoi*
are derived from a Collection is greatly strengthened when
we turn to the second Gospel. Mark shows a decided
partiality to the historic present; yet in ch. iv we find a
series of Sayings—of which the first two (*vv.* 21–23 and
24–25) have only a verbal connection, and the second pair
(*vv.* 26–29 and 30–32) though linked by their common
subject (the kingdom of Heaven), cannot well have been
uttered on a single occasion—preceded in each case by the
formula καὶ ἔλεγε[1]. Now this formula "he used to say" or
"he was saying" is precisely that used to introduce supple-
mentary Sayings of Jewish Rabbis in such a work as the
Pirke Aboth from which Dr Burney[2] quotes as an example
"Hillel said...He used to say...." In the corresponding
Lucan passage (*Luke* viii 16–18) these remarkable intro-
ductions have been improved away. While, therefore, we
are far from possessing complete proof, the character of the
isolated Sayings and the Marcan use of the formula καὶ
ἔλεγε make it probable that here at last we have traces of a
primitive Collection which was used by Mark and by the
compiler of Q or, as we may say, by Matthew in compiling
his *Logia*.

Assuming for purposes of argument that this primitive
Collection is now proved to have existed, what are we to
say of its relation to the Oxyrhynchus Collection? First,
the Egyptian example is not derived from the primitive
document: it is based—as we shall see—on the Gospels
and, indeed, contains elements which are obviously later
than anything in either Matthew or Luke, nor could we well

---

[1] Should *vv.* 2 ff., 9 and 11 be included in this series?
[2] *Ap.* Lock and Sanday, *Two Lectures*, p. 47. See also Taylor,
Oxyrhynchus Logia, pp. 25–6.

xxxiv   *INTRODUCTION*

imagine the Oxyrhynchus Collection to be a recension in the
light of later thought and more developed theology of such
a primitive Collection. Can we then regard these Collections as two links in a chain, and suppose that the inter-
vening links—a greater or less number of other Collections
—have been lost to us? In that case the Oxyrhynchus
Sayings would be, at least indirectly, modelled after the
primitive Collection, and the new matter in them, where
not demonstrably of later date, would acquire a very
weighty claim to historicity. But this is improbable : a
number of Collections covering the period from the earliest
days of Christianity could hardly have perished without
leaving other traces and without the slightest literary
notice[1]. It is far more likely that the Oxyrhynchus Collection was made at a time when the primitive Collection
had been absorbed into the Synoptic Gospels and utterly
forgotten, by some person familiar with the Jewish and
Egyptian practice of treasuring up the pregnant Sayings of
famous teachers. So regarded, it would be but an uncon-
scious revival of the primitive Christian Collection, and its
true model would be Jewish or Egyptian.

§ 4. RELATION TO THE CANONICAL GOSPELS.

The most hasty glance at the text of the two Oxyrhynchus
fragments is sufficient to show that the Collection stood in
intimate, but somewhat peculiar, relation to the Canonical
Gospels. If the nature of this relation can be determined,
we shall have achieved a distinct step towards ascertaining
the position of the Sayings in Christian literature and their
date, and, it may be, we shall find in our hands a clue to
their origin.

In the first place we can say positively that the Sayings
are not extracts from the Canonical Gospels. Some of the

---

[1] Unless indeed λόγοι in *Luke* i 4 be a reference ; though Luke seems
to derive all his *logoi* from Mark or from Q.

Sayings are completely new : others, indeed, approach one
or other of the Gospels very nearly at certain points, but
with such differences as preclude not only the theory of
direct extraction but even of loose citation.

What connection, then, if any, exists between the Oxyrhynchus Collection and the Fourth Gospel? In their
general character the Sayings are clearly Synoptic rather
than Johannine. In the *Prologue*, indeed, we have what
appears to be a direct citation from John ; but this owes
its position to the compiler of the Collection, and therefore
stands quite apart from the Sayings themselves. In fact
the two fragments do not contain a single passage which
can be regarded as derived either from the Fourth Gospel
or from any other Johannine work. And though in 654
(l. 20) I have ventured on a conjecture which lies very
near to a passage in the First Epistle of St John, I do
not suppose that the restoration—should it ever be vindi-
cated—was derived either directly or indirectly from that
work: so impressive a dictum as "we abide in Him and He
in us" cannot have appeared for the first time in St John's
Gospel, but (historicity apart) must have its roots in very
early times; and I do not see why the Oxyrhynchus Collection may not have been indebted to the same source
(whether traditional or documentary) as St John, or to
some nearly related source. At the same time Johannine
influence is distinctly traceable in the Sayings. The most
important mark of this influence is to be found in Saying VIII
(Logion III) where the expression ἐν σαρκὶ ὤφθην αὐτοῖς
distinctly implies, though it need not there consciously
insist upon, the doctrine of Pre-existence, a doctrine which
is quite foreign to the Synoptics: perhaps, too, the mystical
philosophy of the latter part of Saying II (so far as it is
extant) is also to be accounted Johannine. More numerous are expressions and phrases which are characteristic
of the Johannine period. Harnack has remarked that in

Saying VII (Logion II) ὁ κόσμος is used in its Johannine sense of all that is foreign and must remain foreign to the Christian, and if in the same Saying ὄψεσθαι τὸν πατέρα can be paralleled in St Matthew, the Synoptic use of the phrase is altogether exceptional while in St John it is normal. In Saying VIII (Logion III) ἐν σαρκὶ ὠφθῆναι not only indicates a Johannine doctrine, but verbally also is characteristic of the same movement. (Dr Sanday compares 1 *Tim.* iii 16; 1 *John* iv 2; 2 *John* 7.) The use of διψᾶν similarly betrays Johannine influence; but if the view expressed in the Commentary is right, and there is some sort of a literary debt to Isaiah, it marks incipient rather than fully developed Johannism. Finally, Saying X (Logion V), though apparently connected with Matthew so far as form is concerned, is Johannine in spirit (cf. *John* xiv 18; xvi 32).

A fairly definite conclusion may be drawn from these facts: Johannine influence is distinctly present, though definite dependence on any of the Johannine works or literary use of any of them is not likely. Nor is this tendency a vital element in the Sayings, but belongs to their colouring rather than to their substance. On a general view we might say that the Sayings were formed at a period when Johannism was already in the air but still nascent and undeveloped, or if we hold that Johannine thought is essentially the product of one master mind, that they were shaped in a locality which lay back from the stream and was only reached by ripples of Johannine thought.

The relation of the Sayings is therefore with the Synoptics[1]. Of these, Mark may be dismissed at once. There is no Saying which finds a parallel in Mark alone, none whose phraseology is distinctively that of the second Gospel. But with Matthew and with Luke the Sayings are very intimately connected. The first clause of Saying I recalls ζητεῖτε καὶ

---

[1] The relations of the Sayings to the Synoptics are discussed in detail in the Commentary on each Saying.

εὑρήσετε which is common to both Matthew and Luke, and, though it need not be dependent upon either, the probability that it is an amplification of the canonical version is strong. The earlier part of Saying II, though apparently in literary dependence on *Job*, is likely to have been suggested by *Matth.* vi 25 ff., but has a definite point of contact with *Luke* in the phrase ἡ βασιλεία ἐντὸς ὑμῶν ἐστί. On the other hand the ending of Saying III definitely follows *Matth.* xix 30, as against *Luke* xiv 30, while Saying IV is compounded of elements derived from both *Matthew* and *Luke* (Commentary, p. 18). Saying V again seems to be closely parallel to *Matthew* in its substance, and probably in its wording also, though the extreme mutilation of the papyrus forbids a confident conclusion. Saying VI (Logion I) agrees exactly with *Luke* so far as it is preserved. In Sayings VII–IX (Logia II–IV) there is nothing to indicate a direct debt to either *Matthew* or *Luke*, though Saying VII (Logion II), as Harnack has pointed out, contains phrases which are characteristic of the Synoptics. Saying X (Logion V) is certainly connected with Matthew's " Where two or three are gathered together in my name, there am I in the midst," but diverges from it so markedly that the relation may not be immediate. With Sayings XI and XII (Logia VI and VII) we are on firmer ground : the former is undoubtedly connected with *Luke* alone, as is proved by (1) the use of δεκτός, and (2) the manipulation of the physician-proverb; the latter is a contamination of a Saying peculiar to *Matthew*, with elements drawn from the Matthaean version of the parable of the Wise and Foolish Housebuilders.

Such in brief review is the relation between the Sayings and the Gospels. Three conclusions stand out clearly : (1) there are instances of literary dependence on the part of the Sayings upon *Matthew* and *Luke* ; (2) there is no clear trace of Marcan influence ; and (3) Johannine influence has occasionally coloured the Sayings, but is superficial ; and the Sayings are nowhere in literary dependence on the Johannine books.

§ 5. THE NATURE OF THE COLLECTION.

Three main views have been formulated as to the nature and origin of the Oxyrhynchus Sayings. First, they have been thought to constitute a genuine and independent Collection; that is, a Collection of Sayings hitherto current orally and by tradition independently of written documents. On another explanation the Sayings, while containing a large element of accretion due to the mind of their editor (or, perhaps, gathered in the course of tradition), spring ultimately from the Canon. Others regard the Collection as a thesaurus derived from one or more of the uncanonical Gospels.

The first view is based by the discoverers upon two main arguments. (1) "The primitive cast and setting of the Sayings, the absence of any consistent tendency in favour of any particular sect, the wide divergence in the familiar Sayings from the text of the Gospels, the striking character of those which are new, combine to separate the fragment [1] from the Apocryphal literature of the middle and latter half of the second century and to refer it back to a period when the Canonical Gospels had not yet reached their pre-eminent position[1]." (2) The reference to St Thomas in the Prologue of **654** as the authority for the Sayings makes it impossible to believe that the Collection could have been derived from an apocryphal Gospel: such a fraud would have been detected at once[2].

That the Sayings are in some sense primitive is, of course, true; but the epithet is relative, and though the Sayings are undoubtedly primitive as compared with apocryphal literature generally, they are as certainly not primitive when

---

[1] Λόγια Ἰησοῦ, p. 16.　　　　[2] *Ox. Pap.* IV, p. 16.

compared with the Synoptic Gospels—unless indeed the
evidence summed up in the preceding section can be proved
to be misleading. The very divergencies of the Sayings
from their Synoptic parallels point the same way in as much
as they are traceable to the context of the authentic Saying,
or are the result of conflation with another Synoptic Saying
(see especially Sayings IV, XI and XII). Moreover, there
are in the Sayings clear signs of a somewhat later plane of
thought than that of the Synoptic Gospels, signs such as
the sense in which ὁ κόσμος is used in Saying VII (Logion II)
or as the doctrine of Pre-existence implied in Saying VIII
(Logion III). It would indeed be difficult to regard the
Sayings as derived from any documentary source if we could
accept the discoverers' view that according to the *Prologue*
the Sayings were addressed to Thomas, or to Thomas and
one or more other of the disciples. But the Sayings themselves are addressed sometimes in the 2nd person singular,
sometimes in the plural, and are sometimes quite neutral;
and one at least is in answer to a question put by the disciples as a body (Saying V). They can hardly be said to be
addressed exclusively to one (or two) persons. Moreover, in
the Commentary on the *Prologue* I have shown reason for
believing that the Prologue made no such claim to the
authority of Thomas, but merely mentions the apostle in-
cidentally. We cannot, then—at least for the reasons stated
by the first editors—accept the Collection as genuine and
independent.

In view of their common quality, Dr Sanday regards the
Sayings as the work of a single mind, starting as a rule from
a genuine Saying but working it up in a sense of its own:
the individual stamp which they show belongs to a later
generation and to a more developed stage of reflection than
do the authentic Sayings[1]. But while Dr Sanday believes
them to have originated under conditions of thought which

---

[1] *Two Lectures*, pp. 34-35.

the Gospels had created, he considers that direct literary use of the Canonical books is not probable[1].

This view can be accepted as it stands except in so far as it denies the direct literary dependence of the Sayings upon the Gospels. The question has already been considered generally in the section on the Relation to the Canonical Gospels, and the particular instances of dependence are examined in detail in the Commentary: we need only repeat here that literary dependence seems to be the only explanation which will meet the double fact that the correspondences, when they occur, are very close and often extend even to minute points, as in Saying VI (Logion I), and that the divergencies are clearly intentional and calculated either to give a new direction to the Sayings, or (apparently) to adapt it to a new context.

We are now reduced to a choice between two alternatives. Either the Collection is entirely spurious and is a literary invention by a writer of the early second century who set himself to invent Sayings and made some use of Synoptic materials in order to make his work seem genuine; or the Collection is a Treasury of Sayings culled from one or more of the Apocryphal Gospels. The evidence which supports the second alternative excludes the former. Now in an independent Collection (whether spurious or genuine) each Saying must be complete in itself and will reveal no traces of a context: in a Collection of extracts, however, some Sayings may be quite self-contained, but others may be expected to show signs of the context from which they have been torn. The Oxyrhynchus Sayings seem to show such signs of extraction. Saying I is, of course, complete in itself, though we know from Clement of Alexandria that it was actually an extract (see Commentary). The second is too mutilated to admit of absolute certainty, but the question "Who are they who draw us?" postulates a

[1] *Op. cit.* p. 41.

preceding Saying or discourse in which a reference made to
οἱ ἕλκοντες provoked the question. The third Saying (see
Commentary) has all the air of being derived from a narrative
passage parallel to one or other of the Synoptic incidents
dealing with the seeking for precedence. Saying IV is
certainly addressed to an individual—a mark of precision
which is not in the least likely to have survived in a purely
independent Saying—and is therefore to be accounted an
extract: I may perhaps be allowed to draw attention to
my attempt to restore this Saying to its original context.
The discoverers have rightly remarked that the context of
Saying V, which the compiler was obliged to retain in order
to make his Saying intelligible, may be made to furnish an
argument either for or against the theory of extraction[1].
None the less, this Saying is probably an extract: it begins
with a very forcible verb, ἐξετάζουσιν, for which the discoverers
compare *John* xxi 12 οὐδεὶς δὲ ἐτόλμα τῶν μαθητῶν ἐξετάσαι
αὐτόν. The meaning in both cases is more than "to ask
him": it is rather "to examine him strictly," with a view to
clearing up uncertainty or difficulty or mystery. This being
so, we are forced to conclude that the Saying once had
a context representing something to have been said or done
by Jesus which caused the disciples to inquire what was his
precise teaching on prayer, fasting and the like. Saying VI
is addressed in the second person singular; but the use
here may be purely rhetorical, unless the missing first half
gave the extant fragment a new and more particular direction.
But this will not apply to Saying XIII (Logion VIII): here,
as in Saying IV, it seems clear that an individual is addressed,
and we feel a curious sense of incompleteness in the absence
of the circumstances in which the Saying was uttered and
have to paraphrase it in order to understand its meaning.
We should understand better what is signified by 'hearing
with one ear' if we knew for certain what called forth the

[1] *Ox. Pap.* IV, p. 15.

rebuke. The remainder of the Sayings are quite neutral; but the instances in which the loss of a context is more or less clearly indicated are sufficient to create a very strong presumption that the Oxyrhynchus Sayings are in fact extracts.

§ 6. RELATION TO THE APOCRYPHAL GOSPELS.

In the preceding section I have shown reason for believing that the Sayings are extracts; and as they cannot have been derived from the Canonical Gospels, their only possible source is one or more of the Apocryphal Gospels. In this connection Dr M. R. James has suggested that we probably have to do with more than a single source and that several Gospels may have been laid under contribution[1]; but the definite homogeneity of the Sayings alike in style, in method of composition, and in level of thought is fatal to this view which can, indeed, rank as little more than a guess without further precision as to what the plural Gospels were.

It would, perhaps, be generally conceded by those critics who regard the Sayings as extracts that only three of the various sources which have been suggested any longer have a serious claim to consideration—the *Gospel of Thomas*, and the *Gospels according to the Egyptians* and *the Hebrews*[2].

A connection between the Sayings and the *Gospel of Thomas* is somewhat favourably regarded by the discoverers[3] for the twofold reason that in the Prologue the Sayings are attributed to Thomas, and that the Saying "the Kingdom of Heaven is within you" is thought to have occurred in

---

[1] *Contemp. Review*, 1897, p. 157.

[2] Zahn's view that the Ebionite Gospel was the source of the Sayings would be very plausible (compare Saying VII with the *agraphon* quoted by Epiphanius in *Haer.* XXX, 16) were it not that the Christology of that Gospel is irreconcilable with that of Saying X.

[3] *Ox. Pap.* IV, pp. 18–19.

some form in the *Gospel of Thomas* as well as in the
Sayings. The former of these, however, is pure conjecture:
the attribution of the Sayings to Thomas depends on a
restoration of the text of the Prologue which, as I think,
can no longer be maintained; and as I have shown in the
Commentary a more natural and less dangerous supplement
is possible. The second piece of evidence advanced by the
discoverers must also be rejected; first, because Hippolytus[1]
gives no ground for believing that ἡ ἐντὸς ἀνθρώπου βασιλεία
is other than a reference to the well-known Saying in *Luke*
(see Commentary on Saying II); and secondly because the
extant recensions of the *Gospel of Thomas* are confined to
a narrative of the childhood of Jesus and no evidence exists
to show that in its original form the Gospel had any wider
scope, while the Saying about the Kingdom of Heaven cannot have occurred in a narrative of the childhood. And
further, the *agraphon* actually quoted by Hippolytus from
the *Gospel of Thomas* ἐμὲ ὁ ζητῶν εὑρήσει ἐν παιδίοις ἀπὸ
ἐτῶν ἑπτά would seem to indicate that in its original form as
used by the Naasenes this document was no more than a
Childhood-Gospel.

On the other hand Dr Taylor[2] has shown that there are
some points of contact between the Sayings and the extant
versions of the *Gospel of Thomas*. Is it then possible to
maintain with any show of plausibility that the Sayings[3]
which show connection with the Gospel may have actually
been derived from that Gospel in its primitive form? This
must be answered in the negative. Not only is it almost or
quite certain that the original *Gospel of Thomas* was a
Gospel of the Childhood in which most, if not all, of the
Oxyrhynchus Sayings could never have occurred, but the
relevant passages in the extant versions of the Gospel are
so few and so slight, and their contexts are so obviously

---

[1] *Refut.* v, 7.   [2] *Oxyrh. Logia*, pp. 90–93.
[3] See Commentary on Sayings I, VIII and X.

irreconcilable with those of the Sayings which they recall,
that they can be regarded as no more than reminiscences
due directly or indirectly to the Sayings or to their source :
no exercise of ingenuity can make it seem even possible
that Saying VIII (Logion III), for example, took the place
in the original Gospel of the Saying[1] νῦν καρποφορείτωσαν
τὰ σά, καὶ βλεπέτωσαν οἱ τυφλοὶ τῇ καρδίᾳ.

The claim of the *Gospel according to the Egyptians* to be
considered the source of the Sayings has been maintained
by Harnack[2], Badham, Taylor and others. Harnack is
satisfied that the Sayings are extracts, and that their source
was a Gospel of Synoptic type. He goes on to indicate
that the citations[3] in the ps.-Clementine *Second Epistle to the
Corinthians* bear the same relation to the Synoptic Gospels
as do the Sayings in their well-defined dependence upon
Matthew and Luke. All this coincides with the view which
I had formed independently, save only in one particular.
Not only do ps.-Clement's citations resemble the Sayings in
their relation to Matthew and Luke, but also in the peculiar
character of their divergencies from the Synoptic writers[4].
Perhaps the most notable of these citations is the following
(xii 2): ἐπερωτηθεὶς γὰρ αὐτὸς ὁ κύριος ὑπό τινος πότε ἥξει
αὐτοῦ ἡ βασιλεία, εἶπεν· ὅταν ἔσται τὰ δύο ἕν, καὶ τὸ ἔξω ὡς τὸ
ἔσω, καὶ τὸ ἄρσεν μετὰ τῆς θηλείας οὔτε ἄρσεν οὔτε θῆλυ.

This Saying closely resembles the concluding part of a
fragment from the *Gospel according to the Egyptians* quoted
by Clement of Alexandria (*Strom.* III, 9, 64) Σαλώμη φησί·
Μέχρι τίνος οἱ ἄνθρωποι ἀποθανοῦνται;...ἀπεκρίνατο ὁ κύριος·
Μέχρις ἂν τίκτωσιν αἱ γυναῖκες· (*id.* III, 9, 63) ἦλθον [γὰρ]
καταλῦσαι τὰ ἔργα τῆς θηλείας. (*id.* III, 9, 66) Καλῶς οὖν
ἐποίησα μὴ τεκοῦσα;...ἀμείβεται λέγων ὁ κύριος· Πᾶσαν φάγε

---

[1] *Evang. Thom.* A, VIII (ed. Tischendorff).
[2] *Op. cit.* pp. 26 ff.
[3] Preuschen, *Antilegomena*, pp. 32–3.
[4] See esp. Preuschen, p. 32, no. 10.

βοτάνην, τὴν δὲ πικρίαν ἔχουσαν μὴ φάγῃς. (*id.* III, 13, 92) πυνθανομένης τῆς Σαλώμης πότε γνωσθήσεται (γενήσεται: Zahn) τὰ περὶ ὧν ἤρετο, ἔφη ὁ κύριος· Ὅταν τὸ τῆς αἰσχύνης ἔνδυμα πατήσητε καὶ ὅταν γένηται τὰ δύο ἕν, καὶ τὸ ἄρρεν μετὰ τῆς θηλείας οὔτε ἄρρεν οὔτε θῆλυ. But can it be held that ps.-Clement's citation is identical with this fragment? The divergencies between the two are such as can scarcely be reconciled by the theory of quotation from memory.

(i) ps.-Clement's context is purely Lucan: in xii 13 and xviii 18 Luke records inquiries addressed to our Lord by "a certain man"; and in xviii 20 precisely the same question as that recorded by ps.-Clement is asked; though Luke ascribes it to the Pharisees[1]. Contrast this with the fragment from the Egyptian Gospel. Salome inquires: When the things about which she asked shall be known (*or* shall come to pass)? Her question was: "How long shall men die?" This may be ultimately equivalent to "When shall the kingdom of God come?", but formally the two are so remote that it is extremely doubtful if ps.-Clement would have treated them as synonymous. And would he have been likely to have forgotten who put this question? It is vastly more probable that the author of the Egyptian Gospel substituted Salome for the indefinite interlocutor of ps.-Clement's source[2].

(ii) Further, ps.-Clement has nothing to correspond to the remarkable clause concerning trampling upon the garment of shame. It is not likely to have escaped his memory if it stood in his original, and why should he suppress it? So far indeed is the Clementine citation from being identical with the passage from the Egyptian Gospel, that the former appears to stand to the latter rather in the relation of grandfather; for the Gospel-fragment discovered by Grenfell and Hunt (*Ox. Pap.* IV, no. 655, ll. 17 ff.) has a passage which seems to stand between the two under consideration. On the one hand the context λέγουσιν αὐτῷ οἱ μαθηταὶ αὐτοῦ·

[1] See Resch, *Agrapha*, p. 196.   [2] Resch, *op. cit.* 203.

πότε ἡμῖν ἐμφανὴς ἔσει καὶ πότε σε ὀψόμεθα; seems closely
related to the Clementine version[1]; but on the other, the
actual Saying λέγει ὅταν ἐκδύσησθε καὶ μὴ αἰσχυνθῆτε...
betrays kinship with the Egyptian Gospel.

(iii) Again, ps.-Clement has the clause: "and that which
is without as that which is within"—a clause which the
Egyptian Gospel omits. This omission can only be explained
(as I believe) on Resch's theory[2] as deliberate in order to
give a purely Encratite meaning to a Saying whose original
significance[3] was that the kingdom of God will come when
all differences and barriers are broken down.

In view of these divergencies the conclusion that the
Clementine version is not only not to be identified with that
of the Egyptian Gospel but stands at least two stages above
it, seems inevitable. Harnack's argument that the ps.-Cle-
mentine citations were derived from the Egyptian Gospel[4]
rested solely upon the assumed identity of the Clementine
with the Egyptian version : if this may now be taken as dis-
proved, his attribution of the Sayings to the Egyptian Gospel
on the grounds already stated must fall to the ground.

We may add the following considerations : (i) if the passage
in ii Clem. XII 2 were proved to be a loose citation of the
Egyptian Gospel, this would not necessarily imply that all
the citations were from that source; for apart from its context the Saying is rather Pauline than Synoptic. (ii) Though
in view of their common quality the Sayings certainly conform
to one *type*, this need not imply that they necessarily came
from one and the same document. The citation in ii *Clem.*
v 2 may be referred on structural grounds to the *Gospel*

---

[1] Immediately before the citation ps.-Clem. says : ἐπειδὴ οὐκ οἴδαμεν
τὴν ἡμέραν τῆς ἐπιφανείας τοῦ θεοῦ.

[2] Resch, *op. cit.* p. 202.

[3] For the elements in and interpretation of this Saying, cp. Resch,
op. cit. 197 ff.

[4] And, we may add, his theory of the Synoptic character of that Gospel.

according to the Hebrews as I have pointed out elsewhere[1]—
a view which is perhaps strengthened by the fact that it is
immediately followed (in v 5) by an oblique citation of a
passage known to come from that Gospel[2].

Before we leave this matter, however, we must consider
the view of Dr Armitage Robinson[3] who, without committing
himself to Harnack's theory as to the source of the Sayings
as a whole, considers that Sayings VII and X (Logia II
and V) at least may be from the Egyptian Gospel. Clement
of Alexandria[4] in his discussion of the subject of marriage
seems to meet an objection based upon a saying similar to
the first half of Saying X (Logion V), and further on in the
same argument mentions Julius Cassianus as quoting the
Salome dialogue from the Egyptian Gospel. Clement then
quotes the passage from Isaiah dealing with the eunuchs
and their Sabbath-keeping and winds up with an allegorical
interpretation of the eunuchs as keeping Sabbath by refraining
from sin: "Blessed are they," he concludes, "who fast
from the world." Dr Armitage Robinson argues that,
while certainty is impossible, Clement is probably dealing
with not one but three citations from the Egyptian Gospel.
This probability may be admitted; but the admission
does not involve the attribution of Sayings VII and X
to the Egyptian Gospel. As I have tried to show in the
Commentary on the latter of these Sayings, the Saying with
which Clement had to deal had a reference not only to
One and Two, but also to Three which is lacking in the
Oxyrhynchus Saying though it is found in a version quoted
by Ephraem Syrus. If therefore the Saying with which
Clement deals actually occurred in the Egyptian Gospel,

[1] *J.T.S.* XIV, 401–2.
[2] ii *Clem.* V 2 ἡ δὲ ἐπαγγελία τοῦ Χριστοῦ μεγάλη καὶ θαυμαστή ἐστιν
καὶ ἀνάπαυσις τῆς μελλούσης βασιλείας καὶ ζωῆς αἰωνίου.
[3] *Expositor*, 1897, pp. 417 ff.
[4] *Strom.* III, *passim*.

d 2

we may be sure that the Sayings are not derived from that
document, since it is there found in an extended and more
developed form. Neither does it seem likely that Clement's
blessing on "those who fast from the world" is directly
derived from our Saying. If I am not mistaken in my interpretation of Saying VII, Clement's allegorical explanation of
the terms "Sabbath" and the "fast from the world" is
altogether later than the sense in which they are used in the
Saying: and, as I have argued in the Commentary, the
positive beatitude "Blessed are they who fast from the
world" is probably a direct quotation (whether from the
Egyptian Gospel or no), and is therefore not to be identified
with the converse form " Unless ye fast the world, ye shall
not find the kingdom of God" of the Oxyrhynchus Saying.

Lastly, Mr Badham[1] finds that in "their seeming Gnosti-
cism, their asceticism, the country where this papyrus was
discovered, and, above all, some remarkable points of contact
with the *Pistis Sophia* and allied works, no other source
than the Egyptian Gospel seems possible" for the Sayings.
First of all we may dismiss the argument from the place of
origin: hitherto many Gospel fragments have been found in
Egypt but not one which can pretend to come from the
Gospel according to the Egyptians, a work which seems,
indeed, never to have been so very popular in Egypt and
to have been the treasure of a sect rather than of a Church.
As to the alleged asceticism of the Sayings, it is non-existent.
The fast towards the world of Saying VII means no more
than abstention from sin as the thing symbolised in the
rite of fasting, and in Saying V fasting is regarded only as
one of the normal religious observances to be performed
sincerely and without ostentation. Finally, there is the Gnos-
ticism which Mr Badham sees in Saying VIII (Logion III):
"Christ refers back to the days of His flesh in a way which
distinctly implies some occasion between the Resurrection

[1] *Athenaeum*, Aug. 7, 1897.

and Ascension" and "from the '*Pistis Sophia*' and Irenaeus we know what an attraction the Gnostics found in this interval." How unfounded this view is will become clear (I think) to anyone who will weigh the considerations put forward in the Commentary on Saying VIII. I need only repeat here how inappropriate the expression "My soul grieveth over the sons of men" would be in the mouth of the risen Christ.

To sum up. We have now examined the arguments by which Harnack, Robinson and Badham have sought to refer the Sayings to the *Gospel according to the Egyptians*, and as a result we find (*a*) that the passages in the Sayings which have been thought to correspond with citations from the Egyptian Gospel certainly cannot be identified with these citations; (*b*) that while the Egyptian Gospel approached such works as the *Pistis Sophia* in character, the Sayings are strictly of Synoptic type and unmarked by any Gnostic or Encratite traits. In a word, the Egyptian Gospel was certainly not the source of our Sayings.

We turn, then, to the *Gospel according to the Hebrews* which was claimed as the source of the Sayings by Batiffol immediately after the discovery of I. But before we review the evidence which points to this Gospel as the source of our Sayings, we must clear the ground by ascertaining what we mean by the Hebrew Gospel. For Bartlet[1], accepting Dr Sanday's view as to the formation of the Sayings, has taken up a much more advanced position and claims that *Ox. Pap.* I, **654** and **655** are fragments of a Gospel (as opposed to a Collection of Sayings) which is an Alexandrine *Gospel according to the Hebrews* and to be distinguished from the Palestinian Gospel known to Origen and to Jerome.

Now the character of *Ox. Pap.* **655** is quite unmistakeable: it is that of a Gospel in the ordinary sense of the term. Though its matter is wholly discourse, it is continuous.

---

[1] *Contemp. Rev.* 1905, pp. 116 ff.; *Rev. of Theol. and Philos.* I, p. 16.

The change of subject in l. 17 is no more significant than is a new paragraph in the Canonical Gospels; and though it may be argued that the general form of ll. 17–20 corresponds so exactly to that of Saying V as to suggest that that passage is merely one of a string of Sayings, this correspondence proves nothing : it is more likely that Saying V was extracted with its context because of its compact form and because the context was necessary, than that **655** is to be regarded as a string of Sayings merely because one of the Sayings it includes forms with its context an independent paragraph cast in the same shape as the fifth Oxyrhynchus Saying.

The fatal objection to Bartlet's theory, however, lies in another direction. In **654** we have the beginning of a document stated in the Prologue to contain Sayings and not a Gospel (λόγοι : contrast *Mark* i 1), and consisting in a series of Sayings which exhibit only the loosest connection, if any, with one another. Moreover, these Sayings are carefully marked off from one another not only by the introductory formula λέγει Ἰησοῦς, but also by the orthographic coronis and paragraphus. In **I**, a fragment from a point considerably further on in the same document, the critical marks are indeed not found—since **I** belongs to another copy—but the formula λέγει Ἰησοῦς still introduces each saying with that " monotonous regularity " which Dr Bartlet[1] considers so improbable. The natural inference is that since the introductory formula occurs regularly in these two widely separated fragments, it occurred throughout the whole work. Contrast this with the use of **655**. At the end of the discourse (l. 17) a saying is introduced by λέγει alone, while in l. 41—the context is lost—the reproof of the Pharisees is introduced by ἔλεγε. Such a use is quite normal in a Gospel: equally certainly the regularly repeated λέγει Ἰησοῦς of **654** and **I** introducing disconnected apophthegms is

---

[1] *Rev. of Theol. and Philos.* I, p. 16.

foreign to a Gospel unless we are prepared to use that term in a new sense.

Dr Bartlet has also stated what he thinks to be the occasion of his "Gospel"[1]. Holding the Sayings to be post-resurrectional[2], he considers that they were uttered on the occasion mentioned in *John* xx 26 and *Luke* xxiv 44, and that they conveyed the inner meaning of the Sayings uttered during the Ministry. This view seems to be quite arbitrary. (1) The Prologue of **654** does not say—as it might surely be expected to do—that the Sayings were uttered on any such occasion as Dr Bartlet suggests, nor does it affirm that they were addressed to Thomas or to Thomas and others· (2) On the occasion mentioned by Luke it was not the inner meaning of the words of the Ministry that was expounded, but (as is expressly stated in *vv.* 44–6) the Messianic passages of the Old Testament. (3) Dr Bartlet's theory as to the exposition of the "inner meaning" depends wholly upon the connection he sees between the Sayings. Yet there are few critics who can see any such connection, and fewer still who can agree as to its exact nature. Surely if the compiler intended the Sayings to carry an inner meaning, he would not have buried it in such obscurity as to be extracted only by the ingenuity of a modern scholar; more especially as his readers were probably comparatively simple folk. (4) The Sayings themselves do not support the post-resurrection theory. Saying VIII (see Commentary) is not an utterance of the risen Christ, nor does the Prologue indicate such an occasion. All the Sayings are appropriate to the period of the Ministry and to that alone; for who would represent the disciples as asking for instruction as to prayer, fasting and the like in the period which intervened between the Resurrection and Ascension? I conclude, therefore,

[1] *Contemp. Rev.* 1905, pp. 118–9.
[2] Taylor holds the same view as to the occasion of the Sayings, comparing further *Acts* i 3 (*J.T.S.* VII, p. 546).

that **655** is not to be associated with **654** and **1**, and that
these latter are certainly not fragments of a Gospel.

We now come to Dr Bartlet's theory of a twofold *Gospel
according to the Hebrews*, the Alexandrine Gospel known to
Clement of Alexandria, and the Palestinian Gospel of Origen
and Jerome. This theory is built mainly upon the fact that,
although Clement of Alexandria knew no Aramaic, he uses
the Hebrew Gospel familiarly and as a document well
known to his readers[1]. It is therefore presumed that when
Clement describes a Gospel as καθ' Ἑβραίους, the term is
purely descriptive and means "the Gospel in use amongst
the Hebrews" as distinguished from the *Gospel according to
the Egyptians*, that this was no other than that *Gospel
according to the Twelve* which Origen[2] pairs off with the
Egyptian Gospel, and cannot be the Gospel known to
Jerome, since Jerome never shows knowledge of Saying I
and would not have translated the Aramaic Gospel in Greek
had a translation already existed.

This argument cannot, I think, possibly be maintained.
The qualifications καθ' Ἑβραίους and κατ' Αἰγυπτίους are
obviously correlative and can have arisen nowhere else
than in Alexandria, so that we can surely infer that the
Hebrew Gospel was current, at least in Aramaic, in the city
of Clement. Bartlet seems to attach a territorial sense[3] to
these qualifications: it seems much more likely that they
have a sectarian significance, that Αἰγύπτιοι are not really
Egyptians but Jews of Alexandria who had dropped their
own tongue and adopted the language and something of
the philosophic culture of their adopted home[4], and that
Ἑβραῖοι are the more scrupulous Jews of Alexandria who
refused to be absorbed by local influences. The position

---

[1] In *Strom.* v, 14, 96 Clement quotes Saying I, referring to it as ἐκεῖνα.

[2] *Hom. in Luc.* I (Preuschen, p. 1).

[3] As does Harnack, *Altchr. Litt.* II, 1, p. 639.

[4] These would correspond exactly to the Ἰουδαῖοι...οἱ κατοικοῦντες
Αἴγυπτον of *Acts* ii 5–11.

would be exactly paralleled if we compare the Jews of the Ghetto in any of our modern cities with the Jews of the higher financial and commercial classes: the one class excludes the alien culture, faith and manners by which it is surrounded, while the other wholly or partly is eager to assume them. Such a distinction agrees exactly with the different characters of the two Gospels: the one party would evolve the Egyptian Gospel, Gnostic, mystic, and sophistic, and the other, clinging to old customs and rites, would produce the Hebrew Gospel in their own tongue.

That the Gospel καθ' Ἑβραίους is identical with the *Gospel according to the Twelve* mentioned by Origen is in all probability true, but the fact does not indicate two Hebrew Gospels, for Jerome[1] actually mentions "secundum Apostolos" as one of the titles of his so-called Palestinian Gospel.

Again, Bartlet assumes an extraordinary as well as a most unfortunate coincidence when he postulates that Clement chose purely for purposes of distinction a title which all other writers reserve as the special designation of a particular and most important Gospel.

Finally, there remains the difficulty as to Clement's use of an Aramaic Gospel. This difficulty vanishes at once when we recall that an early translation into Greek is *a priori* most probable, and that there is actual evidence in favour of this in the use of the Gospel by Hegesippus, Eusebius, Clement and Origen[2]. That Jerome translated the Gospel from the Aramaic into Greek and Latin indicates no more than that he knew of no other translation: and by his time the *Gospel according to the Hebrews* may well have sunk before the increasing authority of the Canonical Gospels into a position

---

[1] *Contra Pelag.* III, 2.

[2] Harnack, *Gesch. d. altchr. Litt.* II, i, 635–641; *Sitzungber. d. k. Preuss. Akad.* 1904, p. 176. Handmann, *Das Hebräer-Evangelium*, pp. 33, 116–117.

of merely provincial validity—a supposition which would
carry with it the gradual disappearance of the early Greek
rendering. Nor can I see force in the argument that
since Jerome does not quote Saying I, it cannot have
occurred in the Gospel which he translated. It was obviously impossible to quote everything that was remarkable
in that book, and Jerome never attempted to do so: for
neither, it may be observed, does he quote the remarkable
Saying concerning the Division of Souls[1]. As a result of these
various considerations we are now able to claim that when
Clement of Alexandria and Jerome mention the *Gospel
according to the Hebrews*, they are speaking of one and the
same document. We have now to inquire what is the evidence which connects the Sayings with this Gospel.

Our external evidence is limited to the fact that Clement
of Alexandria twice quotes parallels to Saying I, once in an
abbreviated form which he expressly attributes to the *Gospel
according to the Hebrews*, and again in a shape which is
identical in all but minute points with the Oxyrhynchus
version, but this time without naming his source. The question whether Clement's longer or shorter form is the more
exact quotation from the *Gospel according to the Hebrews* is
therefore of great importance: it is discussed in its proper
place in the Commentary on Saying I; but for purposes of the
present argument it will be sufficient to state the conclusion
there arrived at, that Clement's longer form is the more exact:
and this conclusion is, so far as I know, admitted by all critics.

One of the Sayings, then, is certainly derived from the
Hebrews' Gospel. Does internal evidence go to show that the
remaining Sayings are also taken from this source[2]?

In Saying IV the use of the second person singular dis-
tinguishes that fragment of the Mission Charge from the

[1] Preuschen, p. 8, no. 22.
[2] Schmidtke's *Neue Frag. u. Untersuch. z. d. Judenchristl. Evang.*
has come into my hands too late to be of use in the following pages.

Synoptic versions and connects it with the only other known version, the non-canonical fragment quoted by pseudo-Clement[1]. Now this apocryphal fragment exhibits a rhetorical structure which is peculiarly striking and which we find re-peated in a fragment, quoted by Jerome from the *Gospel according to the Hebrews*, and nowhere else. We may there-fore conclude with some degree of confidence that Saying IV also comes from the Hebrews' Gospel[2].

Secondly, the relation of the Sayings on the one hand and of the extant fragments of the *Gospel according to the Hebrews* on the other to the Synoptic Gospels seems to be the same. In the Sayings we found (§ 4) a very strong Lucan influence combined with an almost equally marked depend-ence upon Matthew: Johannine influence was seen to be not essential, being strictly occasional and more a matter of colouring than of form. No clear sign of dependence upon Mark could be detected; but there is an important amount of new matter[3], and some striking results seem due to the author's combination of his sources. How do these features agree with the *Gospel according to the Hebrews*?

The *Gospel according to the Hebrews*, as its alternative title "according to Matthew" shows, must have been very closely allied to our First Gospel. At first sight this predominating Matthaean influence may seem incompatible with the charac-teristic Lucan predominance in the Sayings, but it is not really so. Judging by the extant fragments, we are led to believe that the framework and narrative of this Gospel closely followed that of the canonical Matthew, and to this its subtitle is due. But (to anticipate some of the results of our examination) the apocryphal evangelist made great use of Luke in elaborating or recasting minor incidents, matters

[1] *Ad Corinth.* v, 2–4.

[2] See Commentary on Saying IV and my note in *Journ. Theol. Stud.* xiv, 400 ff.

[3] Some part at least of this may be due to local and oral tradition f (as is likely) the Hebrews' Gospel originated in Palestine.

of detail, and Sayings. Eusebius[1] tells us that the Ebionite readers of the *Gospel according to the Hebrews* "made little account of the rest" : may this not have been because the evangelist had worked into his main "Matthaean" fabric practically all in Luke that was at once striking and acceptable to Jewish converts who would not break wholly with their old faith—and so had robbed Luke of importance? If such were the case it is only to be expected that fragments from the Hebrews' Gospel like the Sayings should show a predominant Lucan influence. Had we their contexts, it is likely that we should find that they occurred mainly in Matthaean settings.

First of all, the extant fragments of the Hebrews' Gospel shows a number of very striking passages in which Lucan influence is incontestable.

(1) The remarkable reproof of the Rich Man quoted by Origen[2] follows Matthew generally in the first half, but later we have : "et ecce multi fratres tui, filii Abrahae, amicti sunt stercore, morientes prae fame et domus tua plena est bonis, et non egreditur omnino aliquid ex ea ad eos." Comparing this with *Luke* xvi 19 ff. we get the following parallels which cannot be accidental : *alter diuitum* (in the first part) at once recalls Luke's "there was a certain rich man"; *filii Abrahae* and *amicti sunt stercore* are the converse of "father Abraham" (*v.* 24) and of "who was clothed in purple and fine linen"; *domus tua plena est bonis* corresponds to "fared sumptuously every day"; *egreditur* is reminiscent of "was laid at his gate" and *morientes prae fame* of "desiring to be fed with the crumbs which fell from the rich man's table." There can be no doubt whatever that the evangelist of the Hebrews' Gospel is here elaborating his main source, Matthew, with reminiscences of the Lucan parable of the Rich Man and Lazarus.

(2) Eusebius[3] has preserved in abstract the parable of the

---

[1] *H.E.* III, 27. 4.

[2] *Comm. in Matth.* XV, 14 (Preuschen, p. 6, no. 11).

[3] *Theophania* (?) (Preuschen, p. 7, no. 14).

Three Servants. One of the servants by a bold departure from the Canonical version is there described as ὁ ἀσώτως ἐζηκώς...ὁ καταφαγὼν τὴν ὕπαρξιν τοῦ δεσπότου μετὰ πορνῶν καὶ αὐλητρίδων. Now the original of the Parable in the Hebrews' Gospel is certainly *Matth.* xxv 14–30 ; but with this has been fused the story of the Wicked Servant of *Matth.* xxiv 48–51 who is remodelled on the lines of the Lucan Prodigal Son. This is clear if we compare the description just quoted from Eusebius with *Luke* xv 13, 30 : διεσκόρπισε τὴν οὐσίαν αὐτοῦ ζῶν ἀσώτως...ὁ καταφαγών σου τὸν βίον μετὰ τῶν πορνῶν.

(3) The fragment describing the appearance after the Resurrection to James[1] has no parallel in Matthew: nor does that Gospel contain anything upon which it can be thought to have been built. The appearance to James is otherwise recorded by St Paul alone[2], and the attestation of this might be thought to be quite the most valuable piece of information preserved to us by the Hebrews' Gospel were it not more than probable that the whole incident is composite. It would appear that the evangelist started from the fact recorded by St Paul and possibly otherwise known ; that James's vow "se non comesurum panem ab illa hora qua biberat calicem domini donec videret eum resurgentem a dormientibus," which can scarcely be historical[3], was suggested by the vow of the fanatics who sought to kill St Paul (*Acts* xxiii 12), and that the remainder of the incident is fashioned after *Luke* xxiv 30, 42 : compare especially Luke's λαβὼν τὸν ἄρτον εὐλόγησε, καὶ κλάσας ἐπεδίδου αὐτοῖς with " tulit panem et benedixit ac fregit et dedit Iacobo iusto." In this case the Lucan influence seems to have radiated from *Acts* as well as from the Gospel.

---

[1] Jerome, *de Viris ill.* 2 (Preuschen, pp. 7–8, no. 18).

[2] 1 *Cor.* xv 7.

[3] If indeed the Synoptics are right in limiting the Last Supper to the Twelve alone. Adeney (*Hibbert Journ.* III, 157) is probably right in seeing here confusion between James the Apostle and James ὁ ἀδελφὸς τοῦ κυρίου.

(4) Jerome[1] states that the Appearance to Peter referred to by Ignatius[2] occurred in the *Gospel according to the Hebrews.* Neither Matthew nor Mark have anything in the slightest degree like this, whereas Luke's account is very close even in some verbal points, as is shown in the following parallel narratives:

<table>
<tr><td align="center">*St Ignatius.*</td><td align="center">*St Luke.*</td></tr>
<tr><td>λάβετε, ψηλαφήσατέ με καὶ ἴδετε ὅτι οὐκ εἰμὶ δαιμόνιον ἀσώματον. καὶ εὐθὺς αὐτοῦ ἥψαντο καὶ ἐπίστευσαν κραθέντες τῇ σαρκὶ αὐτοῦ καὶ τῷ πνεύματι.</td><td>ψηλαφήσατέ με καὶ ἴδετε· ὅτι πνεῦμα σάρκα καὶ ὀστέα οὐκ ἔχει καθὼς ἐμὲ θεωρεῖτε ἔχοντα. καὶ...ἔδειξεν αὐτοῖς τὰς χεῖρας καὶ τοὺς πόδας.</td></tr>
</table>

(5) Finally, there is that incident of the woman "accused of many sins before the Lord" which Eusebius[3] tells us was recorded in the Hebrews' Gospel as well as in the work of Papias. There is little to give a clue to the outline of this episode: it is generally regarded as very similar to or even identical with the famous περικοπή of *John* vii 53—viii 11. On the one hand Eusebius' words γυναικὸς...διαβληθείσης ἐπὶ τοῦ κυρίου certainly point to a situation similar to that in the Fourth Gospel. But the addition ἐπὶ πολλαῖς ἁμαρτίαις goes beyond the version found in John. Is it not likely that while the general outlines of the episode in the Hebrews' Gospel may have corresponded with those in John, they were at least largely coloured by the Lucan account of the woman with the alabastron of myrrh[4]? Compare especially with Eusebius' expression Luke's ἀφέωνται αἱ ἁμαρτίαι αὐτῆς αἱ πολλαί (vii 47).

From the series of passages just examined it appears that the *Gospel according to the Hebrews* contained a very strong Lucan element playing exactly the same part as in the

---

[1] *de Viris ill.* 16.   [2] *ad Smyrn.* III, 1-2.
[3] *H.E.* III, 39. 17 (Preuschen, p. 9, no. 23).
[4] *Luke* vii 37 ff.

Sayings and approximately equal in extent. We must now ask whether the Johannine element which is to be distinguished in the Sayings has a parallel in the Gospel.

(1) Jerome[1] has preserved an account of the Baptism of Jesus which is remarkable both in other respects and especially in its insistence on the rest of the Holy Spirit: "descendit...requievit super eum....Expectabam te ut venires et requiescerem in te. Tu es enim requies mea." In the first place it is evident that the writer is thinking of the dove and the ark (*Genesis* viii 9); that is, that the passage is a product of the age of reflection[2]. And secondly it is to be noted that the Synoptics have nothing like the "requievit...requies" of the Hebrews' Gospel: Matthew has ἐρχόμενον ἐπ' αὐτόν; Mark, καταβαῖνον ἐπ' αὐτόν; Luke, καταβῆναι ἐπ' αὐτόν. John's account alone is parallel: τεθέαμαι τὸ πνεῦμα καταβαῖνον...καὶ ἔμεινεν ἐπ' αὐτόν[3]. Again in the same passage, where all the Synoptics have ἀγαπητός, the apocryphal Gospel has "filius primogenitus," which in its developed theology is nearer to St John's[4] ὁ μονογενὴς υἱός, though for an exact parallel we must go to *Hebrews* i 6; and it must be remembered that the writer is applying *Psalm* lxxxix 27 in a Messianic sense.

(2) The appearance to Peter and those with him quoted above to illustrate the Lucan element in the Hebrews' Gospel shows in one respect a strong development beyond Luke in the direction of Johannism. Luke does not record that the disciples touched Jesus, whereas our Gospel not only states that they touched him, but emphasises the effect which this had upon them[5]. St John's account of the appearance to Thomas, however, is essentially parallel. Is not our evangelist, like St John, combating a form of Docetism?

---

[1] *Comm. in Is.* IV, p. 156 (Preuschen, p. 4, no. 4).
[2] As Adeney remarks on other grounds (*Hibbert Journ.* III, p. 150).
[3] i 32.
[4] i 18: the epithet (πρωτότοκος) is certainly due to *Psalm* lxxxix 7.
[5] Cf. *John* xx 22.

(3) Still more definitely Johannine (though an alien element is also to be felt) is the *logos* cited by Eusebius[1]: "I choose even the good ones [souls] whom my Father in Heaven has given me." It would almost seem as if the compiler of the Hebrews' Gospel were here borrowing directly[2] from St John when we compare *John* xiii 18 ἐγὼ οἶδα οὓς ἐξελεξάμην, and xvii 6 ἐφανέρωσά σου τὸ ὄνομα τοῖς ἀνθρώποις οὓς ἔδωκάς μοι ἐκ τοῦ κόσμου· σοὶ ἦσαν καὶ ἐμοὶ αὐτοὺς ἔδωκας. Yet the context of this Saying was Synoptic: "He taught the cause of the division of the souls which would happen in the houses"—a context which is obviously parallel to *Matth.* x 35–37 ἦλθον γὰρ διχάσαι ἄνθρωπον κατὰ τοῦ πατρὸς αὐτοῦ κ.τ.λ.

(4) Johannine, too, in tone and feeling are such Sayings as that quoted by Jerome[3]: "et nunquam (inquit) laeti sitis nisi cum fratrem vestrum videritis in caritate"; and that reported by the same Father[4]: "ut in evangelio quod iuxta Hebraeos Nazaraei legere consueverunt, inter maxima ponitur crimina qui fratris sui spiritum contristaverit"—even though the second of these may seem to be related to *Matth.* v 22–23.

In the *Gospel according to the Hebrews*, then, there is a distinct Johannine element, but it is by no means deep-seated. There is only a single passage which can possibly be dependent upon St John's Gospel; and in view of our ignorance of St John's sources, it is as likely that in this case both evangelists are reproducing something out of a common stock, as that one is dependent upon the other. So far, at least, the Hebrews' Gospel is parallel to the Sayings. In matters of dogma, it contains the Johannine doctrine of the

---

[1] *Theophan.* IV, 12 (tr. Greissmann) = Preuschen, p. 9, no. 22.

[2] At any rate so close a correspondence will perhaps justify the seeming boldness of my restoration of Saying II, l. 20.

[3] *Comm. in Ephes.* V, 4 (Preuschen, p. 9, no. 21).

[4] *Comm. in Ez.* XVIII, 7 (Preuschen, p. 8, no. 20).

Rest of the Holy Spirit and is anti-Docetic, while Saying VIII in its consciousness of the doctrine of Pre-existence similarly betrays Johannine influence. Yet in none of these matters is dependence on the part of the Hebrews' Gospel or of the Sayings upon John in the least likely. These with the remaining and slighter Johannine touches (such as the use of ὁ κόσμος in Saying VII) observable in the Sayings indicate rather that the fragments of the Hebrews' Gospel together with the Sayings are not widely separated in date from John, than that one is dependent upon the other. In a word, then, the Johannism of the *Gospel according to the Hebrews* is both in its character and its limitations fairly concordant with the Johannine features of the Sayings.

A variety of other considerations contribute to support the case—already a strong one—that the Sayings are taken from the *Gospel according to the Hebrews*.

(1) Unfortunately those writers who have quoted from the Hebrews' Gospel found little or no occasion to cite apophthegms of the type of our Sayings. We cannot therefore be sure how far the new matter in our Sayings was comparable with the new matter in similar Sayings occurring in the *Gospel according to the Hebrews*. Probably, however, it was very much the same: Saying I, on other grounds the strongest link between the Sayings and the Gospel is wholly new, and the fragments of narrative and discourse¹ from the latter which are extant show new matter or new combinations to an extent which makes legitimate the inference that the apophthegms also must have exhibited a similar quality. The loss of these short Sayings is regrettable also because we are unable to say how largely the Hebrews' Gospel employed parallelism. In the Sayings we find this literary feature most prominent: more than half of the thirteen Sayings are parallelistic. Now parallelism is quite a common feature in the Synoptic Gospels, no doubt because it was the form in which short maxims were couched in their sources; but in the Oxyrhynchus

w.   *e*

Sayings we find apophthegms cast in this form although
they are composite : that is, the form has been deliberately
adopted. It can hardly be supposed that anyone but a
Semite writing for Semites would have done this.

(2) Other characteristics in the Sayings point to a source
of essentially Jewish character. The questions asked by the
disciples in Saying V—especially if my restoration of the
fourth be fairly accurate—would be of interest mainly, if not
only, to Jewish converts; and Saying VII (Logion II) deals
with purely Jewish institutions. Could we only accept
Professor Cersoy's conjecture that τὸν κόσμον in that Saying
is a blunder of translation for τὴν νηστείαν this view would
be greatly strengthened, as the reference would then be the
Day of Atonement, and we should be able to recognise one
of the chief traits of the *Gospel according to the Hebrews*—
its attachment to the Old Law[1]. With the matter of institutions we may couple that of language. It has been
thought that traces of an Aramaic original can be found in
the Sayings, and if the truth of this could be shown, it
would go far to prove that they were derived from the
Hebrews' Gospel which was in Aramaic[2]. Yet such traces
may originate a stage further back, in the period of oral
rather than of documentary currency ; and in some cases
they may be no more than Semiticisms in the Alexandrine
or Palestinian κοινή. Unfortunately the instances in which
such peculiarities have been thought to occur are never
definite. In Saying VII (Logion II), as we have just seen,
Cersoy shows that our actual reading τὸν κόσμον may be a
translator's error for τὴν νηστείαν (the original being either
Hebrew or Aramaic). The same scholar points out that in

[1] Eusebius, *H.E.* III, 27. 4.

[2] I am inclined, however, to suspect that this Gospel was composed
in Greek—the version used by Clement of Alexandria—but was almost
at once rendered in Aramaic, perhaps in deference to national prejudice ;
and that this *original* Greek version was then lost. But I have not tried
to mature or to test this view.

Saying X (Logion V) the injunction "raise the stone," which has caused some difficulty, may be again a mistranslation for "hew the stone"; but such an emendation postulates a Hebrew original. Again in Saying XI (Logion VI) Cersoy notes that ποιεῖ θεραπείας suggests an Aramaic original— though the recurrence of the idiom in the *Protevangelium* (xx) makes it more like a mere Semiticism current in the κοινή—and that γινώσκοντας αὐτόν is again the blunder of a translator from the Aramaic for εἰς τοὺς γνωστοὺς αὐτοῦ. Harnack has further pointed out that the use of καί...καί is a Semitic feature. No one of these instances[1], however, forces us irresistibly to the conclusion that the Sayings were translated from Aramaic, and the matter must be left as an open question.

(3) In the Commentary on the Sayings we have noted frequent instances of the use of Jewish literature. In Saying II the mention of birds, beasts and fishes as symbolical of creation and as a link between Man and Heaven is almost certainly to be connected with *Job* xii 7–8, or perhaps with *Psalms* viii. Saying VIII (Logion III) opens with an adaptation in a Messianic sense of *Baruch* iii 28; its use of δυψᾶν and μεθύειν in a spiritual sense is likely to be due to *Isaiah* lv 1 and xxiii 1, while the phrase πονεῖ ἡ ψυχή derives from *Isaiah* liii 10. The ninth Saying (Logion IV) seems to make use of a traditional Jewish Saying to be found in the *Pirke Aboth*: and the second part of the same Saying undoubtedly is related to *Eccles.* x 9. The conflation of two New Testament elements in Saying XII (Logion VII) is due to *Isaiah* ii 2, and the "high hill" of that Saying seems to be inspired by *Isaiah* xxviii 4. Such a use of Jewish literature is what might be expected

[1] To these should be added the idioms πονεῖ ἐπί and υἱοὶ ἀνθρώπων in Saying VIII (Logion III): the repeated use of καί throughout the Sayings to introduce new clauses might be an Egyptian feature; for in Coptic narratives clauses are commonly introduced by ⲟⲩⲟϩ, 'and.'

in fragments which (as we are urging) came from a Gospel
designed for Jewish readers. How far, then, do the known
fragments of the *Gospel according to the Hebrews* show a
corresponding use of Hebrew literature?

1. The Baptism fragment which we have already noticed
as containing a Johannine element certainly looks back to
Genesis viii 9, the dove and the ark being regarded as symbolical of the Holy Spirit and Our Lord. It is important to
notice that this Messianic interpretation corresponds exactly
to the application of *Baruch* iii 28 in Saying VIII. But the
literary affinities of this passage extend further[1]. The idea
of the *rest* of the Holy Spirit is derived primarily from
Isaiah xi 1 "the Spirit of the Lord shall rest upon him";
while the words "tu es enim requies mea" not uncertainly
echo *Psalms* cxxxii 14 "This is my rest for ever: here will
I dwell, for I have desired it"; and lastly "tu es filius meus
primogenitus" are inseparably connected with *Psalms* ii 7
"Thou art my son," and *Psalms* lxxxix 27 "And I will
make him my first-born."

2. Origen[2] quotes a remarkable fragment from the Story
of the Temptation found in the *Gospel according to the
Hebrews*. Matthew, it will be remembered, narrates the
beginning of the Temptation in the simplest way: "Then
was Jesus carried up by the Spirit into the wilderness[3]."
But the *Gospel according to the Hebrews* with characteristic
boldness and love of novelty represents Our Lord himself
as telling the story of his Temptation, and puts into his
mouth these startling words: ἄρτι ἔλαβέ με ἡ μήτηρ μου τὸ
ἅγιον πνεῦμα ἐν μιᾷ τῶν τριχῶν μου καὶ ἀπήνεγκέ με εἰς τὸ ὄρος
τὸ μέγα Θαβώρ. The expression "my mother the Holy

[1] The important parallels which follow were pointed out by Dr
Armitage Robinson (*Expositor* v, p. 194).
[2] *Comm. in Joh.* II, 12. 87 (Preuschen, *Antilegomena*, p. 5, no. 5).
[3] IV, 1.

Spirit" does not immediately concern us¹; but the remainder is beyond doubt a literary loan. Thus in Ezekiel² we have ἀνέλαβέ με τῆς κορυφῆς μου καὶ ἀνέλαβέ με πνεῦμα ἀναμέσον τῆς γῆς καὶ ἀναμέσον τοῦ οὐρανοῦ, and in *Bel and the Dragon*³ καὶ ἐπιλαβόμενος αὐτοῦ ὁ ἄγγελος Κυρίου τοῦ ᾿Αμβακοὺμ τῆς κόμης αὐτοῦ τῆς κεφαλῆς ἔθηκεν αὐτὸν ἐπάνω τοῦ λάκκου τοῦ ἐν Βαβυλῶνι. One, probably both, of these passages was imitated by the author of the Apocryphal Gospel. Even the reference to Tabor is not without significance. Dr Adeney⁴ points out, indeed, that it was occupied in the time of Our Lord by a Roman fortress and so was unsuitable⁵ as a site for the Temptation, but considers that *Psalms* lxxxix 12 and *Jeremiah* xlvi 18 suggested the reference.

3. The Evangelist elaborates in characteristic fashion the account of one of the signs which followed the Crucifixion. Matthew⁶ says simply that at the last cry of Jesus the Veil of the Temple was rent in twain; but the *Gospel according to the Hebrews* (as rendered by Jerome⁷) gives "superliminare templi infinitae magnitudinis fractum esse atque divisum." Once again the change seems to be due to literary imitation dictated by a desire to find fulfilments of as many Messianic passages as possible; for the original is *Isaiah* vi 4, where the LXX⁸ has ἐπήρθη τὸ ὑπέρθυρον ἀπὸ τῆς

¹ The Ophites (see Irenaeus I, 28. 1) held that the Spirit was feminine (grammatically the *word* is feminine in Semitic languages) and was beloved by the First Man to whom she bare a Son. See Resch, *Agrapha*, p. 382.

² viii 3.   ³ v 36.   ⁴ *Hibbert Journal* III, p. 162.

⁵ But may not the Roman fortress have been regarded as roughly reproducing "Babylon" and the "den"? In such a neighbourhood, too, something might be seen of the "kingdoms of the world and the glory of them."

⁶ iv 1.

⁷ *Comm. in Matth.* XXVII, 51 (Preuschen, *Antilegomena*, p. 7, no. 17).

⁸ The Hebrew of Isaiah does not give the same parallel: the A.V. renders "the posts of the door," the R.V. "the foundations of the threshold." From this it appears that the author of the *Gospel according*

φωνῆς ἧς ἐκέκραγον (doubtless the *Gospel according to the Hebrews* had something parallel to the κράξας φωνῇ μεγάλῃ of *Matth.* xxvii 50).

In their use of Jewish literature, then, the Sayings and the fragments of the *Gospel according to the Hebrews* are parallel; and in this we have one of the strongest supports for our attribution of the Sayings to this Gospel.

4. The conflation of elements or expressions from different Gospels or from different parts of the same Gospel is one of the most salient features in our fragments of the Oxyrhynchus Collection (see Commentary on Sayings I, II, III, IV, X, XI and XII), and in this again it corresponds exactly with the *Gospel according to the Hebrews*. Thus in the earlier[1] of the two fragments of the Baptism-narrative the opening words "ecce mater domini et fratres eius" at once recall *Matth.* xii 46 ἰδού, ἡ μήτηρ καὶ οἱ ἀδελφοί, and are grafted on to the general narrative of the Baptism. Again, in the dialogue on forgiveness between the Lord and Peter[2], the words "in die" are derived from Luke, while the "septuagies septies" belongs to Matthew. But the most striking example of this method of composition is the incident of the Rich Man[3]. Here the main Matthaean framework has been filled in with material taken, as we have already seen in detail, from the Lucan parable of the Rich Man and Lazarus. And similarly in the story of the Three Servants[4], one of the Matthaean characters is remodelled on the lines of the Lucan Prodigal Son. As in

to the *Hebrews* used the LXX (see Dr Armitage Robinson in *Expositor* v, 198 ff.); but Jerome (*de Vir. ill.* ch. 3) says that the "Hebrew Matthew" followed the Hebrew of the O.T. and not the LXX. Nestle (*Evang. Kirchenbl. f. Würt.* 1895, no. 16), however, gives reason for thinking that the Hebrew for "lintel" is more original than that for "veil" (the latter being a variant). If so, the Evangelist need not be supposed to have used the LXX.

[1] Preuschen, p. 4, no. 3. [2] *Ib.* p. 6, no. 10.
[3] *Ib.* p. 6, no. 11. [4] *Ib.* p. 7, no. 14.

its use of the Old Testament, then, so also in its method of composition and in its use of existing Gospels, the *Gospel according to the Hebrews* shows the same features as do our Sayings.

We may now sum up the results of this somewhat lengthy review of the evidence connecting the Sayings with the *Gospel according to the Hebrews.* The only Saying which can be positively identified as a quotation is from the *Gospel according to the Hebrews.* The peculiar relation of the Sayings and of the Gospel to the Synoptics and to the Fourth Gospel are identical. Moreover in their parallelism, in their interest in matters such as would only concern Jewish converts, in their use of Semitic idioms and syntax, and perhaps even in traces of an Aramaic original, the Sayings postulate a source of Semitic character. Both documents, finally, are exactly parallel in the method and extent of their use of Hebrew literature, and in the peculiar method of their composition from conflated elements. Positive proof we cannot have, unless some new discovery should hereafter add to our evidence; but this at least we may claim, that circumstantial evidence in abundance and from every side points to the conclusion that the Oxyrhynchus Sayings are excerpts from the *Gospel according to the Hebrews.*

§7. THE DATE OF THE COLLECTION.

The discoverers date **1** "not much later than the beginning of the third century," and **654** to the middle or end of the same century: they consider, therefore, that the Collection as such must go back at least to the end of the second century, but, in view of internal evidence, consider that it is likely to have been formed before A.D. 140. Since the papyri belong to the third century and one, at least, of them to the earlier half of it, we may accept the first part of Grenfell and Hunt's conclusion, that the Collection must have been formed not later than the end of the second century. But can we carry the date further back? The Sayings themselves seem to carry tolerably distinct marks of their relative, though perhaps not of their numerical date : they are later than both Matthew and Luke in that they draw upon both these Gospels, and since these Gospels must have taken some years to become generally current, they must be decidedly later. At the same time they are obviously products of the true, if later, Synoptic age. On the other hand, if the view expressed above as to the Johannine element in the Sayings is true, the Sayings are somewhat earlier than the Fourth Gospel. While we find in the Sayings something of Johannine phraseology and dogma, these are both limited in extent and rudimentary in development. The natural inference then is that the Sayings belong to a period when the Synoptic tendency had not yet failed, but when Johannine influence—of which the Fourth Gospel marks the acme—was still only nascent. Now Messrs Grenfell and Hunt take the step back from 200 A.D. to 140 A.D. or earlier relying on their theory that the Collection is essentially independent, a theory which permits them to date the Collection by the internal evidence of the Sayings. In our view, however, the Sayings are extracts ; and if this is correct, the date of the formation of the Collection cannot be fixed from the character of the Sayings themselves. The Prologue, which dates from the formation of the Collection, furnishes us with one clue in the use of a citation from St John, allowing us to infer that the Collection was made at a period when the Fourth Gospel was already accepted as of universal authority. This, however, is but vague and would admit the possibility that the Collection was formed at quite a late date. Fortunately the *Prologue* gives another indication which is of the highest value. The compiler describes his work as containing οἱ λόγοι οὓς ἐλάλησεν Ἰησοῦς and he prefaces each Saying with λέγει Ἰησοῦς. Now even in Luke the substitution of ὁ κύριος for the name Ἰησοῦς is growing marked and towards the end of the second century becomes the normal method of reference to Our Lord. The heading of the *Didache*, which is perhaps the nearest parallel we have to the Prologue of the Sayings, begins not Διδαχὴ Ἰησοῦ but Διδαχὴ τοῦ κυρίου. The use of the name Ἰησοῦς, then, both in the Prologue and in the introductory formula may be taken as a sign of distinctly early date, and we may conclude, though on different grounds, that Grenfell and Hunt's date, A.D. 140, is the latest that is likely for the formation of the Collection.

§8. THE PURPOSE OF THE COLLECTION.

The problem of the purpose of the Collection is not altogether distinct from the question of its origin. If, for example, it could be proved that the Sayings are totally disconnected and possessed of no common quality, it would be extremely probable that the Collection was a mere record intended to preserve Sayings which were in danger of being lost, simply because they were Sayings of Jesus. Two main views—apart from the discoverers' view that it is a genuine collection—have been taken as to the purpose of the Collection: some critics consider that they had a didactic purpose, and therefore were connected by a continuous thread of subject or idea: others fail to see any connection, or any continuous connection, between the Sayings, and regard them simply as a record. This second point of view is adopted by the discoverers who consider that, prior to the formation of the Collection, the Sayings were current in tradition and were gleaned up here and there. They admit, of course, that in **654** the first four (? three) Sayings are linked by the idea of the Kingdom which recurs in each, but point out that with Saying V the interconnection ceases altogether, and that it is in any case unlikely that such a link could have been maintained throughout a long series

of Sayings. In 1 the discoverers confess themselves totally
unable to trace any thread of connection.

This is indeed the only logical conclusion which can be
reached, if indeed the Sayings are to be taken at their face-
value. Other critics, however, have preferred not to do this
and consider that the Sayings are mere texts covering an inner
and connected meaning and are not to be interpreted literally.

(1) Mr Badham[1] traces the connection as follows:
"[Wouldst thou see Christ? ...] Purify thine eye by self-
examination (Saying VI). Purify thine eye by abstinence
from the world and by observing times of tranquil meditation
(Saying VII). Remember how satiety blinded the world when
I came (Saying VIII). If thy home be godless, go forth and
find me in the stocks and stones of the desert (Saying X).
Forsake thine uncongenial Nazareth (Saying XI). Look up to
where the lights of thy true home are burning (Saying XII)."
He therefore takes the fragment to be "a page from some
middle-Christian 'Garden of the Soul'." The main objection
to this allegorical interpretation is that there is nothing to
warn us that such is intended, although we now possess the
Prologue to the Collection as a whole. The Sayings are there
stated to be merely "lifegiving words of Jesus," and the plain
man would naturally take them at their face-value as such
and no more. Mr Badham's result, in fact, is only attained
by putting into the Sayings much more than is actually to
be found in them: take, for instance, his interpretation of
Saying X. It urges, in effect, "Seek loneliness: it is the
best way to find Christ"; whereas the real meaning of the
Saying is "In spite of loneliness, Christ is ever present."
Nor can I think that this "inner meaning" adds to the
value which the Sayings already possess as independent units.

(2) Dr Bartlet[2] also finds an inner meaning in the Sayings,
which he considers to be a collection of texts forming the

---

[1] Writing on 1 (*Athenaeum*, Aug. 7, 1897).

[2] *Athenaeum*, July 24, 1897; *Rev. of Theol. and Philos.* I, pp. 13-14.

basis of a manual of instruction designed, perhaps, like the
Two Ways of the *Didache* for catechumens prior to Baptism.
I is held to come from the close of the series of Sayings to
which it belonged : "The earlier pages have presumably set
forth the nature of the Kingdom of God....Then come the
conditions of true receptivity ; and the thought proceeds
thus :—To judge aright one must purge one's own eye.
Only he who cultivates an unworldly spirit can find God's
kingdom : to see the Father, one must not neglect to observe
the Sabbath in spirit and in truth. Incarnate wisdom testifies
sadly to the unreceptiveness of the mass ; but speaks cheer
to the solitary soul amid the faithless many—ever near though
hidden from the careless, superficial eye. That his own in
Judaea have not believed should be no stumbling block : it
is according to rule. Yet in spite of present fewness believers
are bound to hold out and make themselves felt at last,
because firm-built on the very Mount of God." Here, as in
Mr Badham's paraphrase, connection is attained—if indeed
it is attained—only by reading into the Sayings what is not
there and what is not even hinted at. But is unity of thought
really attained ? On Dr Bartlet's interpretation Saying VI
inculcates right judgment ; Saying VII, unworldliness and
Sabbath keeping ; and Saying VIII complains of the unreceptiveness of men. The Sayings surely break up into
separate units as they were before. And certainly it would
be difficult to establish connection between two such Sayings
as the eighth and tenth, where the words "I found *all* men
drunken and *none* found I athirst" are followed by "where
there is one alone, I say I am with him."

The attempt, then, to trace a thread of connecting thought,
which constitutes the didactic purposes of the Collection,
must be abandoned. The first three Sayings do indeed
deal with the kingdom, but can these be thought to provide
a sufficient basis for an adequate treatment of the subject of
the kingdom, more especially as Saying I asserts that the

kingdom is reached through seeking, finding and amazement, while Saying II declares that the kingdom is within
us and is to be attained by self-knowledge[1]? When the
compiler therefore grouped the first three Sayings together,
he did so because they were concerned with the same
subject, and not in order to provide a compendium of
scriptural teaching on the Kingdom of Heaven : had that
been his aim, he would doubtless have devoted many more
Sayings to the subject. I believe, then, that the order of
the Sayings is almost fortuitous : here and there a catch-
word may have led the compiler to group together Sayings
which happened to deal with one subject[2]; but there is no
connecting thread of thought running through the whole.
At the same time, if the Sayings are—as we hold—extracts,
the compiler must have selected them because of some
quality which they possessed. This quality, I believe, was
made clear in the Prologue and I would refer to the Commentary for my reasons for this conviction. But apart from
my restoration of "life-giving" as the epithet applied by the
compiler to the " words of Jesus " which he collected, the
Sayings one and all are of the type known in modern
devotional works as " helpful." It is hard to see any
connection between the Sayings, but their individual value
is clear. If, then, we regard the Sayings as having been
selected for their independent worth and not as units
illustrating any developing principle, as a thesaurus designed
to give in a small compass[3] so much of a Gospel as was

[1] Dr Lock (*Ch. Quarterly Review*, LVIII, 425) thinks *truth* is the idea
which links the first five Sayings. In I, however, the idea depends upon
a restoration; in II and IV, it is not obvious, but (at most) latent; it is
hard to see how it can enter into III at all, and only in V is it explicit.

[2] It should be noted that while Sayings I–III deal with the kingdom,
the same subject is brought up again in Saying VII many pages further
on : this does not seem to indicate an orderly arrangement such as is
required by the theory of arrangement on a definite principle.

[3] A small book of Sayings, we should remember, could be searched

judged most likely to be of help and comfort in daily life, does not this view agree best with the data on which we have to work?

§ 9. THE FORMULA λέγει Ἰησοῦς.

Each Saying in the Collection is preceded by the words λέγει Ἰησοῦς, a form which has given rise to much discussion. Consequently it will be well to begin by clearing the ground. And first, these words are not part of the excerpt (if we hold the Sayings to be excerpts), since it is inconceivable that such a series of selected passages should all happen to begin with an historic present and not occasionally with εἶπε or ἔλεγε. For the same reason it is impossible to regard these words as narrative connections in what is really part of a Gospel (as opposed to a series of distinct Sayings). The phrase, then, is a formula introducing each Saying. This formula, however, is decidedly remarkable, and no parallel is readily forthcoming. We are familiar with such a prefatory phrase as λέγει αὐτῷ (or αὐτοῖς) ὁ Ἰησοῦς in the Fourth Gospel and, less frequently, in the Synoptics; but the absolute use without a dative is certainly most unusual. Probably the Synoptics have no parallel; and in St John's Gospel only xi 39 and xiii 31 (to which may be added the absolute εἶπεν ὁ Ἰησοῦς of vi 9) readily present themselves. How is this general suppression of the dative to be explained? The first, perhaps, and most important consideration in the compiler's mind was the need to keep his formula from passing into a vague context: had he added αὐτῷ or αὐτοῖς or a personal name like τῷ Πέτρῳ to the simple λέγει Ἰησοῦς, he would no longer have the advantage of a formula, and would feel more and more the necessity for enlarging his

through in a very short time, whereas it would take long for the devotee in search of consolation to find in his copy of a Gospel—whether roll or codex—the particular Saying which should satisfy his need.

rudimentary context by adding when or in what circumstances
the Saying was spoken to such and such persons.

What, then, was the compiler's object in repeating this
formula with such regularity? Partly, no doubt, it is due
to the influence of the Jewish Collections of Sayings where
two or more Sayings of one teacher are introduced thus:
"A. said…. He used to say…." But this fails to explain the
regularity with which the personal name and the present
tense is repeated. We may to some degree account for this
regularity on the grounds of literary propriety: just as the
Sayings could not be strung together one after another
without any formula at all, so it was in a literary sense
impossible to preface each Saying with a mere ἔλεγε or
καὶ ἔλεγε: only in a short series would such a form of introduction be tolerable. The formula chosen, λέγει Ἰησοῦς,
however, most successfully avoids this danger. With each
new Saying it demands and rouses our attention afresh, and
its effectiveness can best be understood if by way of experi-
ment we substitute ἔλεγε…καὶ ἔλεγε…καὶ ἔλεγε. But beside
the literary motive there was also, no doubt, a feeling that
the incisive repetition of the formula added to the solemnity
with which the Sayings sound.

Lastly, what is the significance of the present tense λέγει,
since its unvarying use shows that it cannot be regarded as
an ordinary historic present? Dr Burney[1] has suggested that
the present tense may have been adopted by a translator from
neo-Hebrew or Aramaic who found a participle alone in
his original, and that a participle might be expected if the
formula represents the formula of citation used in the Talmud.
This explanation may account for the repeated present tense,
but I am by no means clear that it accounts for the repeated
personal name, and am still more doubtful that the Collection
as such ever existed in any other language than Greek[2].

[1] *ap.* Lock and Sanday, *Two Lectures,* pp. 47–8.
[2] The Prologue seems to reproduce the exact wording of St John except
where the writer found it necessary to adapt the citation to his period.

Dr Lock[1] somewhat favours the suggestion that the present tense is used because Jesus was still living when the Collection was made by some disciple; but apart from the difficulty noticed by Dr Lock in applying this to Saying VIII, there are so many points in which the Sayings are obviously later than the Synoptic Gospels that this explanation is quite inadmissible. Dr Lock considers Swete's suggestion that the formula is parallel to the common λέγει ἡ γραφή where a sacred book is cited as a present witness to the truth, but rejects it "as inappropriate in a disconnected series of Sayings which are not apparently illustrative of any one truth." The best and, as I believe, the true solution of the difficulty is to explain the present as having a mystical force[2]. Dr Lock very happily cites in illustration the verse from Cowper's hymn: "Jesus speaks and speaks to thee," and an incident from Dr Pusey's *Life*; and this is confirmed by the Prologue to the Collection with its marked insistence on the fact that Jesus lives. If the author of the *Epistle to the Hebrews* could write of Abel (XI 4) καὶ δι' αὐτῆς (*sc.* πίστεως) ἀποθανὼν ἔτι λαλεῖ, we can surely conclude that when he wrote λέγει Ἰησοῦς the compiler of the Collection meant that the Sayings were not to be regarded as words uttered in the past and only historically interesting, but as being ever repeated[3] by that Jesus "who lives and appeared to the Ten and to Thomas."

The formula uses Ἰησοῦς not ὁ Ἰησοῦς. In this, I think, we have another mark of Johannine influence in the compiler of the Collection. In the Fourth Gospel ὁ Ἰησοῦς is

[1] *Two Lectures*, p. 18.

[2] At the same time the historic use of the present in Gospel narrative (such as *John* xi 39 λέγει ὁ Ἰησοῦς...λέγει αὐτῷ ἡ ἀδελφή...(40) λέγει αὐτῇ ὁ Ἰησοῦς...(44) λέγει αὐτοῖς ὁ Ἰησοῦς) is likely to have contributory influence.

[3] The sentiment is somewhat that of *Hymns Anc. and Mod.* 207, "And His that gentle voice we *hear*, | Soft as the breath of even, | That *checks* each fault, that *calms* each fear, | And *speaks* of heaven."

the normal mode of reference, but Ἰησοῦς (without the article) is by no means uncommon (see *John* iv 47, 50; viii 1, 49, 54, 59; xii 44, 54; xviii 34; xix 26). In the Synoptics, on the other hand, Ἰησοῦς is very rare. Personages referring to Jesus may indeed say Ἰησοῦς (see *Matth.* xxvii 17, 22; *Mark* v 7; as also in *John* i 46, ix 11); but otherwise ὁ Ἰησοῦς seems to be always used in the narrative after Jesus had entered on his ministry: *Mark* i 9 and *Luke* iii 21; iv 1, [4] significantly fall within the narrative of the Baptism and Temptation[1].

---

[1] But *Luke* iv 8, 13 (Temptation) uses ὁ Ἰησοῦς.

THE PROLOGUE

οὗτοι οἱ {οι} λόγοι οἱ [ζωοποιοὶ οὓς ἐλά-]
λησεν Ἰη(σοῦ)ς ὁ ζῶν κ[αὶ ὀφθεὶς τοῖς δέκα]
καὶ Θωμᾷ. καὶ εἶπεν [αὐτοῖς· πᾶς ὅστις]
ἂν τῶν λόγων τούτ[ων ἀκούσῃ, θανάτου]
οὐ μὴ γεύσηται.   5

1. ΟΙΤΟΙΟΙΟΙ, P: οὗτοι οἱ {οι}, Swete, Heinrici, Taylor: {οι} τοῖοι οἱ,
GH, Wessely: ζωοποιοί, Bruston: θαυμάσιοι, GH: θαυμαστοί, Lock:
ἀληθινοί, Swete, Taylor: ἔσχατοι, Hicks: τελευταῖοι, Wilamowitz:
ἐκλεκτοί, ἐκλελεγμένοι Heinrici: ἀληθεῖς, Batiffol.   2. καὶ ὀφθεὶς τοῖς
δέκα, Ed.: κύριος or καὶ ἀποθανών, GH: κύριος τοῖς τε ἄλλοις (or τοῖς ι')
μαθηταῖς, Bartlet: καὶ ὁ κύριος, Heinrici: …Ἰούδᾳ τῷ | καὶ Θωμᾷ, Lake:
καὶ ἀληθινός, Lock: καὶ μένων Φιλίππῳ, Bruston: κρυφίως Φιλίππῳ,
Batiffol: καὶ δόξα αὐτοῖς καὶ θαῦμα, Wessely: κατενώπιον Ματθίᾳ (?),
Wilamowitz.   3. αὐτῷ ὁ κύριος· ὅστις, Swete: διδάσκων· ἐάν τις, Lock:
αὐτοῖς· ἀμὴν λέγω, Taylor.   1–5. τοῖοι οἱ λόγοι οὓς ἐλά|λησεν Ἰησοῦς ὁ
ζῶν Κηφᾷ | καὶ Θωμᾷ. καὶ εἶπεν· μακάριος ὃς | ἂν τῶν λ. τούτων ἀκούσῃ,
θανάτου | ο. μ. γ.: Hilgenfeld.

These are the life-giving Sayings which Jesus spake who
liveth and was seen of the Ten and of Thomas. And He said to
them: Whosoever heareth these Sayings shall not taste of
death.

1. οὗτοι οἱ [οι] λόγοι. The first
syllable[1] is certainly ΟΙ (with an ι,
and not with a damaged γ as Heinrici and Taylor supposed). GH
consider the possibility of the correction οὗτοι, but prefer to omit
the initial syllable and to read τοῖοι
οἱ. The insertion of a superfluous
initial syllable, however, seems
very doubtful, whereas an ad-
ditional ΟΙ may well have crept
in after ΟΥΤΟΙ ΟΙ. The correction

of Swete and Heinrici is certainly
more natural than τοῖοι = τοιοίδε,
supported though this is by late
prose use, and is strengthened by
the parallel οὗτοι οἱ λόγοι μου οὓς
ἐλάλησα πρὸς ὑμᾶς[2] quoted by the
discoverers; and to this—remem-
bering that the 'Prologue' is in
reality no more than a diffuse title
—we may add Baruch i 1 καὶ
οὗτοι οἱ λόγοι τοῦ βιβλίου οὓς ἔγραψε
Βαρούχ.

[1] Ox. Pap. IV p. 4.   [2] Luke xxiv 44.

ζωοποιοί. Such restorations as those of Hicks and Wilamowitz are impossible since most if not all the Sayings are demonstrably pre-resurrectional. The Prologue—as a Prologue—has every appearance of aiming at the terse and forceful, and on this ground epithets like 'wonderful,' 'true,' and the rest, must be discarded. Swete, indeed, suggests ἀληθινοί, comparing *Apoc.* xxii 6 οὗτοι οἱ λόγοι πιστοί καὶ ἀληθινοί; but the epithet used attributively, as here, is weak. Something like ζωοποιοί seems to be required[1]. The phrases ὁ ζῶν and θανάτου οὐ μὴ γεύσηται make the idea of *life* very prominent in the Prologue, and the second of these especially seems to be intended to make good some claim made by the Editor for the Sayings. This claim must have been conveyed in the lost epithet of λόγοι, and ζωοποιοί seems most suitable. Parallels are plentiful : *John* vi 63 τὸ πνεῦμά ἐστι τὸ ζωοποιοῦν...τὰ ῥήματα ἃ ἐγὼ λελάληκα ὑμῖν πνεῦμά ἐστι καὶ ζωή; *Psalms* cxviii (cix) τὸ λόγιόν σου ἔζησέν με; *Barnabas* vi οὕτω καὶ ἡμεῖς τῇ πίστει τῆς εὐαγγελίας καὶ τῷ λόγῳ ζωοποιούμενοι ζήσομεν; lastly, the Fourth Gospel concludes (xx 31) with a claim exactly similar to the claim of the Prologue : ταῦτα δὲ γέγραπται ἵνα πιστεύσητε...καὶ ἵνα πιστεύοντες ζωὴν ἔχητε ἐν τῷ ὀνόματι αὐτοῦ[2].

2. The restoration of this line is of the greatest importance, since here and in l. 3 all editors find a declaration of the ultimate authority for the Sayings, and consider that this, whether true or false, has an important bearing on the origin of the Collection.

The published conjectures[3] deal with two points which are, or seem to be, more or less distinct : (*a*) What followed ὁ ζῶν? (*b*) Who was coupled with Thomas? All editors take it as granted that Θωμᾷ depends on ἐλάλησεν.

(*a*) GH[4] suggested—but with equal reserve in both cases—κύριος or καὶ ἀποθανών, and Swete[5] prefers the latter of these, for which cf. *Apoc.* i 18. Heinrici[6] thinks ὁ ζῶν καὶ κύριος a likely solution, but finds the expression only in Gnostic writings. Lock[7] supports his ὁ ζῶν καὶ ἀληθινός by reference to the Litany of Sarapion :—ὁ θεὸς ...ὁ τὸν χαρακτῆρα τὸν ζῶντα καὶ ἀληθινὸν γεννήσας; but ἀληθινός was probably chosen in that passage as an appropriate epithet for χαρακτήρ rather than as ordinarily connected with ὁ ζῶν.

(*b*) Who was associated with Thomas? GH[8] suggested Philip or Matthias, as the *Pistis Sophia* represents these with Thomas as recipients of a special revelation; and Batiffol and Bruston followed this suggestion. Professor Lake's brilliant conjecture[9] Ἰούδᾳ τῷ | καὶ Θωμᾷ has the advantage of leaving Thomas' authority for the Sayings undivided, and is supported by the Ἰούδας ὁ καὶ Θωμᾶς of the *Acta Thomae*. All these proposals, however, are checked by an insuperable obstacle—the fact that the use of one (or two)

---

[1] When I proposed this (*J.T.S.* xiii 74) I was unaware that Bruston had already made the same suggestion (*Fragm. d'un anc. recueil de Paroles de Jésus* p. 13).

[2] Compare further *Apoc.* xxii 18 seq. ; ps.-Athan. Λόγος Σωτηρίας X. (*ad init.*) ὦ μακαρία ψυχή, ἡ ἀκούσασα τούτους τοὺς λόγους...καὶ ποιοῦσα. μαρτύρομαι παντὶ τῷ ἀκούοντι τὰ ῥήματα ταῦτα καὶ ποιοῦντι, ὅτι τὸ ὄνομα αὐτοῦ γραφήσεται ἐν τῇ βίβλῳ τῆς ζωῆς.

[3] The reading καὶ Θωμᾷ is almost universally admitted. Wessely alone (*P.O.* iv p. 161) reads κ[αὶ δόξα αὐτοῖς] καὶ θαῦμα; but the original does not bear out this suggestion, which in itself is unsatisfactory.

[4] *Ox. Pap.* iv p. 4.
[5] *Expos. Times* xv 490.
[6] *Theol. Stud. u. Kritiken* 1905 p. 192.
[7] *Ch. Quarterly Rev.* lviii p. 426.
[8] *Op. cit.* p. 4.
[9] *Hibbert Journ.* iii p. 339.

names distinctly excludes the main body of the Apostles. We cannot assume that the Editor meant otherwise any more than that Barnabas[1] writing γέγραπται ἐν τοῖς δέκα λόγοις ἐν οἷς ἐλάλησεν... πρὸς Μωσῆν meant that others than Moses received the Ten Commandments. Yet if we judge of the Sayings—as we must—by their Synoptic parallels, we must conclude that neither were they the fruit of private revelation, nor have they any connection with Thomas : Saying v offers the most obvious proof of this point. The difficulty is so real that Swete[2] is driven to think that the Prologue is the opening of one of twelve groups of Sayings each of which was conventionally attributed to one of the Apostles, citing the title of the *Didache*, Διδαχὴ κυρίου διὰ τῶν δώδεκα ἀποστόλων τοῖς ἔθνεσιν, and suggesting that the real title of the Oxyrhynchus Collection may have been Λόγοι Ἰησοῦ πρὸς τοὺς δώδεκα. Bruston[3] takes a desperate position maintaining that the Prologue is really the colophon to a preceding section of 'Words of Eternal Life' addressed to Philip and Thomas,—a theory which the arrangement of the papyrus alone puts out of court. Nor is the difficulty which we are discussing surmounted by Bartlet's τοῖς τε ἄλλοις or τοῖς ἰ μαθηταῖς | καὶ Θωμᾷ. This restoration singles out Thomas (presumably as the recorder of the Sayings) without excluding the rest of the Apostles : cf. *John* xx 26 ἦσαν ἔσω οἱ μαθηταὶ αὐτοῦ καὶ Θωμᾶς μετ' αὐτῶν, *Mark* xvi 7 εἴπατε τοῖς μαθηταῖς αὐτοῦ καὶ τῷ Πέτρῳ. But it is hard to see why Thomas should be claimed as the recorder of Sayings with which tradition has never connected him :

and if the Editor really claimed the authority of Thomas, he would surely have done so categorically. We are therefore driven to doubt that the dependence of Θωμᾷ on ἐλάλησεν is inevitable. Two passages suggest another form of restoration. *Mark* xvi 11 κἀκεῖνοι ἀκούσαντες ὅτι ζῇ καὶ ἐθεάθη ὑπ' αὐτῆς ἠπίστησαν, and *Acts* i 3 παρέστησεν ἑαυτὸν ζῶντα...ὀπτανόμενος αὐτοῖς[4]. In each case the statement that Jesus lives is followed immediately by quotation of proof : he was seen by such and such persons. These passages together with *John* xx 26 (quoted above) suggest the restoration given in the text[5], which makes the reference to Thomas natural and easy. The Editor, thinking, doubtless, of the appearance to Thomas as recorded by St John, says in effect : ' These are the words of One who lives now and once gave proof of his immortality by appearing not only to the Ten, but even to the Apostle who had most strongly declared his scepticism.' The sharply marked present and aorist participles (cp. *Mark* xvi 11, quoted above) contrast, of course, a continuous, permanent state and a past, momentary action respectively.

3. The restoration of the first half of the lacuna, though not of the greatest importance, is interesting. The discoverers proposed αὐτοῖς, and this is perhaps the most acceptable : it involves the assumption, indeed, that the Editor has made a mistake (since in *John* viii 48 sqq. the Saying is addressed to the Pharisees) ; but such an assumption is reasonable enough on general grounds and is supported by the verbal errors in the Saying itself. Doubtless he was quoting from memory. The αὐτῷ of Swete

---

[1] xv. [2] *Op. cit.* p. 494.
[3] *Fragm. d'un anc. recueil de Paroles de Jésus* p. 12.
[4] See further 1 *Cor.* xv 4–8 : *Luke* xxiv 34.
[5] Alternatives are καὶ φανεὶς τοῖς δέκα and καὶ φανερωθεὶς τοῖς ἰ.

cannot be accepted. If right it would imply that the quotation is from a document, now lost, in which the Saying was actually addressed to Thomas; for the substitution of a definite person, Thomas, for the Pharisees as addressee could only be accounted for by the theory of defective memory.

Lock would supply διδάσκων, in imitation of the 'citation-formula' of St Paul and Clement of Rome. But, as I have tried to show in the Introduction, the Prologue is something very different from that formula, if indeed it can properly be called a formula.

While reading αὐτοῖς in the Text, I venture to suggest αὐτός, believing that emphasis may account for the peculiar position of the pronoun[1]. In this connection it will be well, at the risk of partial repetition, to consider the whole train of thought of the Prologue. I have already argued that *life* is the dominant note, and if the conjectured epithet of the Sayings, 'life-giving,' is right, it was natural for the Editor to develop, enforce, and justify the implied claim. If I am not mistaken, the following paraphrase will represent his idea: ' These are the life-giving words of Jesus —life-giving, because they were spoken by one who lives for ever, as he proved by appearing after his death and burial to his disciples, so that even the most sceptical was convinced. And Jesus himself and no other claimed precisely this virtue for his words.' In such a form the Prologue is at least rid of the dangerous and extremely difficult claims to the authority of Thomas, while the

thought seems reasonable and apposite. The Prologue, then, is, as I have said, no more than a diffuse title or head-line like *Mark* i 1 or *Baruch* i 1 (quoted above); but the Editor was carried away into a vindication of the claim he had made for special quality of his Collection.

One point of some interest remains to be examined. What relation does the citation (ll. 3–5) bear to its Johannine parallel? The passage in question (*John* viii 51–52) is as follows: ἀμήν, ἀμήν, λέγω ὑμῖν· ἐάν τις τὸν λόγον τὸν ἐμὸν τηρήσῃ, θάνατον οὐ μὴ θεωρήσῃ εἰς τὸν αἰῶνα. εἶπον αὐτῷ οἱ Ἰουδαῖοι ...καὶ σὺ λέγεις ἐάν τις τὸν λόγον μου τηρήσῃ οὐ μὴ γεύσηται θανάτου εἰς τὸν αἰῶνα. The Jewish perversion of the Saying is decidedly closer to the version in the Prologue than is the actual Saying. It is probable, as we have seen, that the Editor is actually quoting from the Fourth Gospel[2]: how, then, are we to explain the divergencies? GH[3] note that in the Synoptics (*Matth.* xvi 28, *Mark* ix 1, *Luke* ix 27) θανάτου γεύεσθαι denotes physical death ; and Dr Taylor is certainly right in saying[4] that in the Johannine parallel the Jews perverted the Saying 'he shall not die spiritually' (θ. οὐ μὴ θεωρήσῃ) into 'he shall not die physically' (θ. οὐ μὴ γεύσηται). The citation in the Prologue is therefore erroneous as it stands. But the error seems due simply to uncritical quotation from memory. The Editor failed to perceive the distinction between the two expressions, and perhaps the Synoptists had made the second phrase the more familiar to him. Similarly, inexact memory and

---

[1] Cf. *Mark* iv 27 ὡς οὐκ οἶδεν αὐτός.
[2] The Prologue (the work of the Editor of the Collection) is of course later than the actual Sayings, and therefore stands on a different level in its relation to the Canonical Gospels.
[3] *Ox. Pap.* IV pp. 3–4.   [4] *Oxyrh. Sayings* p. 4.

confusion will adequately explain
the use of ἀκούσῃ (which is, of course,
certain) for St John's τηρήσῃ : cp.
John v 24 ὁ τὸν λόγον μου ἀκούων...
ἔχει ζωὴν αἰώνιον. τούτων seems to

be an adaptation, made consciously
or unconsciously to apply the
Logion directly to the Sayings of
the Collection.

SAYING I

λέγει Ἰη(σοῦ)ς·
μὴ παυσάσθω ὁ ζη[τῶν τοῦ ζητεῖν ἕως ἂν]
εὕρῃ, καὶ ὅταν εὕρῃ [θαμβηθήσεται, καὶ θαμ-]
βηθεὶς βασιλεύσει, κα[ὶ βασιλεύσας ἀναπα-]
ήσεται.

6. ζητῶν τὴν ζωὴν ἕως ἄν, GH: τοῦ ζητεῖν, Heinrici: ἐκζητεῖν or τὴν
σοφίαν, Taylor: τὴν ἀλήθειαν, Lock: τὸν πατέρα, Swete: τὸν κύριον,
Bruston: με..., Batiffol.   6-9. μὴ παυσ. ὁ ζ. ἕως ἂν | εὕρῃ· καὶ ὅταν
εὕρῃ θαμ|βηθεὶς β. καὶ ἀναπα|ήσεται, Hilgenfeld.   7. θαμβείσθω,
Swete.   8. ΒΑCΙΛΕΥCΗ, P.

Jesus saith :
Let not him who seeketh cease from seeking until he hath found ;
And when he hath found, he shall be amazed ;
And when he hath been amazed, he shall reign ;
And when he hath reigned he shall have rest.

This Saying is quoted with very
slight divergencies by Clement of
Alexandria[1], so that the restoration
of the discoverers is, in all essen-
tials, certain. As they observed, a
word not quoted by Clement must
have followed ζητῶν and must have
been either an object or something
dependent upon παυσάσθω[2]. They
suggested tentatively τὴν ζωήν,
which is not unattractive. But the
verb θαμβεῖσθαι gives the impression that something less abstract
is required—something which will

produce *amazement.* Lock's τὴν
ἀλήθειαν[3] and Taylor's τὴν σοφίαν
seem too frigid and trite. The
former supports his conjecture by
reference to the *Clementine Homilies* (III 52): διὸ καὶ ἐκβόα λέγων·
δεῦτε πρὸς ἐμὲ πάντες οἱ κοπιῶντες·
τουτέστιν οἱ τὴν ἀλήθειαν ζητοῦντες καὶ μὴ εὑρίσκοντες αὐτήν...
καὶ ἄλλοτε· ζητεῖτε καὶ εὑρίσκετε,
ὡς μὴ προδήλως κειμένης τῆς ἀληθείας.   But in this passage it seems
unlikely that the homilist is interpreting two familiar Sayings by

[1] *Strom.* II 9. 45 (quoted below, p. 7, *q.v.*).
[3] *Ch. Quart. Rev.* LVIII 422.

[2] *Ox. Pap.* IV p. 5.

means of a third and less known utterance: the explanation has rather the air of being his own. And the supplement is too long for the lacuna. Swete's τὸν πατέρα and Bruston's τὸν κύριον (for which cp. *Isaiah* lv 6) chime ill with what follows: it is a little too obvious to say that to find the Father will cause amazement.

Moreover, these restorations, if accepted, would make it hard to understand why Clement should have omitted a positive object such as 'truth' or 'wisdom.' But Clement may well have dropped out some word or phrase which was slightly redundant and seemed to him to carry no particular weight: Heinrici's τοῦ ζητεῖν is exactly such a phrase and has therefore been adopted in our text.

It may be objected that this leaves the meaning of the clause too indefinite: what is the object or aim of search? The answer is, that no precise definition of the object sought was intended. The search is that vague aspiration of humanity after something above and beyond itself—the ἀποκαραδοκία τῆς κτίσεως of *Romans* viii 19. To a pious Jew of the Old Dispensation this aspiration might embody itself in the expectation of a Messiah (cp. *Luke* ii 25), though this specialized form of the idea is, of course, far narrower than the spirit of the present Saying. It is, in fact, the fulfilment of the vague, instinctive longing or aspiration of mankind—in Pauline phrase the revelation[1] of the glory which is to be—which provokes amazement, a condition of mind necessarily preceding ability to partake in the Kingdom itself.

Harnack understands θαμβηθήσεται in the sense of joyful surprise, comparing the Parable of the

Hidden Treasure (*Matth.* xiii 24). This parallel exactly illustrates the transition between εὑρεῖν and θαμβεῖσθαι, though θάμβος should rather mean *awed* amazement[2] as in *Luke* v 9 : ἐξῆλθε ἀπ᾽ ἐμοῦ κτλ. θάμβος γὰρ περιέσχεν αὐτόν; *Mark* xvi 5 ἐξεθαμβήθησαν (of the women at the Sepulchre).

The Saying as a whole is new, but every part of it falls into line with the Synoptic record of the teaching of Jesus. The first clause is close enough to the familiar ζητεῖτε καὶ εὑρήσετε of *Matth.* vii 7 and *Luke* xi 9 ; and the discoverers also quote *Matth.* vi. 33 ζητεῖτε δὲ πρῶτον τὴν βασιλείαν [τοῦ θεοῦ]. For the second stage we have no such verbal parallel. Yet the sense is quite in harmony with the Synoptic account. Amazement, as Harnack remarks, follows finding in the Parable of the Hidden Treasure[3]; and the same Parable covers the third clause also, for in both amazement is followed by enjoyment of the thing found. The final clause echoes the promise of *Matth.* xi 28 δεῦτε πρός με...κἀγὼ ἀναπαύσω ὑμᾶς : to come to Christ is synonymous with attaining the Kingdom, and both the First Gospel and the Saying promise rest to those who do so.

In l. 7 Swete has proposed to read θαμβεῖσθω as shorter than the future (which the discoverers regard as somewhat long for the space to be filled), and because the imperative is used in the initial clause. This seems unnecessary: the future is apparently possible graphically—and an error such as θαμβήσεται is quite possible,— and the context surely requires it. Wonder follows upon finding as a natural consequence and not as a state to be induced.

---

[1] *Romans*, viii 18.   [2] See Swete *Exp. Times* xv 491.

[3] Joy is a concomitant of finding in the Parable because of the nature of the thing found.

ll. 8–9. ἀναπαήσεται is a vulgar form of ἀναπαύσεται : it occurs in the parallel Clem. Alex. *Strom.* II 9 45, and *Apoc.* xiv 13[1]. The popularity of the saying is proved by the number of parallels in patristic and apocryphal writings. The most important of these are two citations by Clement of Alexandria:

(1) *Strom.* II 9 45 ταύτης δὲ (sc. τῆς ἀληθείας) ἀρχὴ τὸ θαυμάσαι τὰ πράγματα, ὡς Πλάτων ἐν Θεαιτήτῳ λέγει (p. 155 D) καὶ Ματθίας ἐν τοῖς Παραδόσεσι παραινῶν · ' θαύμασον τὰ παρόντα ' ᾗ κἂν τῷ καθ' Ἑβραίους εὐαγγελίῳ ' ὁ θαυμάσας βασιλεύσει ' — γέγραπται — ' καὶ ὁ βασιλεύσας ἀναπαήσεται.'

(2) *Strom.* V 14 ἴσον γὰρ τούτοις (Plato *Tim.* p. 90) ἐκεῖνα δύναται · ' οὐ παύσεται ὁ ζητῶν ἕως ἂν εὕρῃ · εὑρὼν δὲ θαμβηθήσεται · θαμβηθεὶς δὲ βασιλεύσει · βασιλεύσας δὲ ἐπαναπαυθήσεται.'

Two questions now arise : (*a*) which of these two citations is the more faithful quotation from the *Gospel according to the Hebrews*? (*b*) Is the more exact citation independent of or identical with our Saying?

(*a*) It is probable that the former passage is a substantial and not a verbal quotation from the Gospel. Clement is putting the Platonic doctrine that wonder begets knowledge : assuming for the moment that the longer version is that which was actually found in the Gospel, may we not fairly argue that Clement would have reduced it to the short form found in *Strom.* 11? For the first two clauses of the longer form would be omitted as irrelevant ; and θαυμάσας would be substituted for θαμβηθείς, because the latter, while essential in the citation as such, was unsuitable to Clement's application of it—θάμ-

βος being an emotion which occupies the mind exclusively and therefore not conducive to receptivity. We may remark also that the longer version is far more Synoptic in style[2] than the shorter.

While, therefore, absolute certainty is impossible, it seems in the highest degree probable that Clement's shorter version is a modification—made by himself— of the longer form, and that the longer form is the true citation from the Hebrew gospel.

(*b*) In what relation, then, does the longer form stand to the present Saying ? In Clement we have οὐ παύσεται—εὑρών—ἐπαναπαυθήσεται for the μὴ παυσάσθω—ὅταν εὕρῃ—ἀναπαήσεται of the Saying. Such variants as these which carry with them no difference of meaning are such as occur naturally wherever quotation is made from memory. They are common enough in early Christian literature to justify us in treating the instances under consideration as negligible, and consequently deciding that the Oxyrhynchus Saying is identical with a Saying recorded in the *Gospel according to the Hebrews*. Further, in the Introduction, as also at various points in the Commentary, reason has been shown for regarding the Sayings as extracts. Coupling, then, the conclusion that the Sayings are extracts with the identity of Saying 1 and Clement's citation from the *Gospel according to the Hebrews*, we reach the important conclusion— which, I believe, is universally admitted, that Saying 1 is quoted from the *Gospel according to the Hebrews*.

The other citations are less direct, and for the most part do little more than show how popular the Saying was. (1) *Clement* 11 6

[1] Cp. Heinrici *op. cit.* p. 194.
[2] As we should expect a citation from the *Gospel according to the Hebrews*. For the climax-form cp. *Matth.* v 25.

ἡ δὲ ἐπαγγελία τοῦ Χρίστου μεγάλη καὶ θαυμαστή ἐστιν καὶ ἀνάπαυσις τῆς μελλούσης βασιλείας καὶ ζωῆς αἰωνίου. Resch thinks this passage is dependent on Clement *Strom.* II 9; but in any case the passage unmistakably refers to the last clause of the Saying: Taylor[1] believes that θαυμαστή proves reference to the preceding clause also, a view which would oblige us to regard the passage as confirming Clement's shorter citation as the genuine form. But to say 'the promise is wonderful' is very different from saying 'the promise is attained through wonder,' as the Saying does. 'Clement' doubtless uses θαυμαστή without any reference to our Saying[2]. (2) *Acta Thomae* (ed. Tischendorf) οἱ ἀξίως μεταλαμβάνοντες τῶν ἐκεῖ ἀγαθῶν ἀναπαύονται καὶ ἀναπαυόμενοι βασιλεύσουσιν. Though ἀνάπαυσις and βασιλεία are reversed, it is clear that here again the reference is to the final clause of the Saying. (3) *Evang. Thomae* (ed. Tischendorf) A. v. ἀρκετόν σοί ἐστι ζητεῖν καὶ μὴ εὑρεῖν. This passage has not hitherto been connected with

the Saying. It seems to mean 'It is bad enough that, with all your search (expectation) as a pious Jew for the Messiah, you have failed to recognise him when he is before you. Do not make it worse by ill-treating me,' and so agrees exactly with the explanation of the initial clause in our Saying given above. (4) It seems at least possible that in *Pistis Sophia* (§ 251 ed. Petermann) there is an adapted version of Saying I: Schwartz's translation of the Coptic is as follows: 'et dicite iis: ne remitte quaerere per diem et noctem, et ne ανακτε (?=ἀνέχετε) vos usque dum inveneritis μυστήρια purgatores quae purgabunt vos ut reddant vos εἱλικρινές lumen, ut euntes in altitudinem κληρονομήσητε lumen mei regni.' If we leave out the Gnostic dressing of this passage, the remainder *ne remitte quaerere... usque dum inveneritis...ut euntes in altitudinem* κληρονομήσητε (lumen) *mei regni*, is obviously very close to the Oxyrhynchus Saying; indeed the first clause of the Coptic is verbally almost identical with the first clause of the Greek.

SAYING II

λέγει Ἰ[ούδας· τίνες ἄρα]
οἱ ἕλκοντες ἡμᾶς, [καὶ πότε ἐλεύσεται]   10
ἡ βασιλεία ⟨ἡ⟩ ἐν οὐρα[νοῖς οὖσα; λέγει Ἰη(σοῦ)ς·]
τὰ πετεινὰ τοῦ οὐρ[ανοῦ, καὶ τῶν θηρίων ὅ-]
τι ὑπὸ τὴν γῆν ἐστ[ιν ἢ ἐπὶ τῆς γῆς, καὶ]
οἱ ἰχθύες τῆς θαλά[σσης, οὗτοι οἱ ἕλκον-]
τες ὑμᾶς· καὶ ἡ βασ[ιλεία τῶν οὐρανῶν]   15
ἐντὸς ὑμῶν [ἐ]στι· [καὶ ὅστις ἂν ἑαυτὸν]

[1] *O.S.* p. 6.
[2] Cp. Hippol. *Comm. in Dan.* IV 60 τοῦ οὖν κυρίου διηγουμένου...περὶ τῆς μελλούσης τῶν ἁγίων βασιλείας ὡς εἴη ἔνδοξος καὶ θαυμαστή.

γνῷ ταύτην εὑρή[σει· καὶ εὑρόντες αὐτὴν]
ἑαυτοὺς γνώσεσθε [ὅτι υἱοὶ καὶ κληρονόμοι]
ἐστε ὑμεῖς τοῦ πατρὸς τοῦ π[αντοκράτορος, καὶ]
γνώσ⟨εσ⟩θε ἑαυτοὺς ἐν[θ(ε)ῷ ὄντας καὶ θ(εὸ)ν ἐν ὑμῖν.] 20
καὶ ὑμεῖς ἐστε ἡ πτό[λις θ(εο)ῦ].

9 ff. λέγει Ἰησοῦς· ἐρωτᾶτε τίνες οἱ ἕ. ἡμᾶς εἰς τὴν βασιλείαν εἰ ἡ β. ἐν
οὐρανῷ ἐστιν;.........τὰ π. τοῦ οὐρανοῦ καὶ τῶν θηρίων ὅτι ὑπὸ τὴν γῆν
ἐστιν ἢ ἐπὶ τῆς γῆς καὶ οἱ ἰ. τῆς θαλάσσης, οὗτοι οἱ ἕλκοντες ὑμᾶς, καὶ ἡ
βασιλεία τῶν οὐρανῶν ἐντὸς ὑμῶν ἐστι καὶ ὅστις ἂν ἑαυτὸν γνῷ ταύτην
εὑρήσει.........ἑαυτοὺς γνώσεσθε καὶ εἰδήσετε ὅτι υἱοί ἐστε ὑμεῖς τοῦ πατρὸς
τοῦ παντοκράτορος...γνώσ⟨εσ⟩θε ἑαυτοὺς ἐν...............καὶ ὑμεῖς ἐστὲ
ηπτρ......, *GH*.

λ. Ἰησοῦς· μὴ φοβείτωσαν οἱ ἕ. ὑ. ἐπὶ τῆς γῆς· ὑμῶν γὰρ ἡ β. ἐν
οὐρανῷ, καὶ ἐφ' ὑμῖν ἔσται τὰ π., *Bartlet*.

λ. Ἰησοῦς· ἐρωτᾶτε τίνες οἱ ἕ. ἡμᾶς ἄνω εἰς οὐρανὸν εἰ ἡ β. ἐν οὐρανῷ
ἐστιν; ἀμὴν λέγω, *Taylor*.

λ. Ἰησοῦς· τίνες εἰσιν οἱ ἕ. ὑ. πρὸς τὴν βασιλείαν; ἡ β. ἐν οὐρανῷ· οἱ
δὲ ἐπὶ τῆς γῆς καὶ τὰ π. τοῦ οὐρανοῦ καὶ πᾶν κτίσμα ὅτι ὑ. τ. γ. ἐστιν καὶ
ἐν τῷ ἄδη καὶ οἱ ἰ. τῆς θαλάσσης, οὗτοι οἱ ἕλκοντες ὑμᾶς, *Swete*.

λ. Ἰησοῦς· πῶς λέγουσιν οἱ ἕ. ἡμᾶς εἰς τὰ κριτήρια ὅτι ἡ β. ἐν οὐρανῷ
ἐστιν; μήτι δύναται τὰ π. τοῦ οὐρανοῦ ἐπιγιγνώσκειν τί ὑπὸ τὴν γῆν
ἐστιν; καὶ τί ἐν τῷ οὐρανῷ οἱ ἰ. τῆς θαλάσσης; οὕτως οἱ ἕλκοντες ὑμᾶς.
καὶ ἡ βασιλεία ὁμῶς μέντοι ἐντὸς ὑμῶν ἐστιν, καὶ ὃς ἐὰν τὰ ἐντὸς ὑμῶν
γνῷ, ταύτην εὑρήσει............ἑαυτοὺς γνώσεσθε ἐνώπιον τοῦ θεοῦ. καὶ υἱοί
ἐστε ὑ. τοῦ π. τοῦ τελείου ἐν οὐρανῷ. γνώσεσθε ἑαυτοὺς ἐνώπιον τῶν
ἀνθρώπων, καὶ ὑ. ἐστε, ᾗ πτοεῖσθε, *Deissmann*.

λ. Ἰησοῦς· μὴ λέγητε, διατί οἱ ἕ. ἡ. εἰς τὴν γῆν ἐπειδὴ ἡ β. ἐν οὐρανῷ
ὑπάρχει· μήποτε τὰ π. τοῦ οὐρανοῦ λέγουσιν διατί ὑ. τ. γ. ἐστιν ἑρπετὰ ἢ
διατί οἱ ἰ. τῆς θαλάσσης; τοῖοι οἱ ἕλκοντες ὑμᾶς· καὶ ἡ βασιλεία τῶν οὐρανῶν
ἐ. ὑ. ἐστι. ὅστις οὖν ἑαυτὸν γνῷ ταύτην εὑρήσει καὶ ὅταν ὑμεῖς ἐ. γνώσεσθε,
εἰδήσετε ὅτι υἱοί ἐστε ὑ. τ. π. τ. παντός, καὶ ὅταν γνώσεσθε ἐ. ἐκ θεοῦ,
τότε οὐράνιοι καὶ ὑμεῖς ἐστε η (?) πτεροφόροι, *Bruston*.

λέγει Ἰ. · τίνες οἱ ἕλκοντες ἡμᾶς εἰσιν; ἡ β. ἐν οὐρανῷ καὶ τὰ π. τοῦ
οὐρανοῦ. τί ὑπὸ τὴν γῆν ἐστιν; οἱ ἰ. τῆς θαλάσσης ἕλκοντες ὑμᾶς. καὶ ἡ
βασιλεία ἐντὸς ὑμῶν ἐστιν. ὃς ἂν ἑαυτὸν γνῷ ταύτην εὑρήσει. ἑαυτοὺς
γνώσεσθε· ὑμεῖς ἐστε τοῦ π. τοῦ τελείου. γνῶσθε ἑαυτοὺς ἐν αὐτῷ. καὶ
ὑμεῖς ἐστε ἡ πτόα, *Hilgenfeld*.

λ. Ἰησοῦς· αἰτεῖτε, *Lock* : λ. Ἰησοῦς· μὴ εἴπητε, *Bartlet*.

9–11. λέγει Ἰησοῦς μὴ φοβείτωσαν οἱ ἕ. ὑ. εἰς κριτήρια· ὑμῶν γὰρ ἡ β.
ἐν οὐρανῷ, *Wessely*.

17. εὑρήσει· ἐὰν γὰρ ἀληθῶς, *Swete*: εὑρήσει καὶ εὑρόντες αὐτήν,
Heinrici.   18. ΓΝωCΕCΘΑΙ, *P*, corr. *GH*: υἱοὶ καὶ θυγατέρες, *Swete*.
19. ὑψίστου· καὶ ὑμεῖς ὅταν, *Bartlet*.   20. ἐν τῇ πόλει τοῦ θεοῦ, *Blass*:
ἐν τῷ πατρὶ ὑμῶν, *Heinrici*: ἐντὸς τῆς πόλεως ὄντας, *Swete*: ἐν τοῖς
ἑαυτοῦ ὄντας, *Taylor*.   21. ἡ πτόλις, *Blass*, *GH*, *Swete*: ἠπτημένοι,
Heinrici: ἡ πτόλις θ(εο)ῦ, *Bethune Baker*.

Judas saith: 'Who, then, are they who draw us? And when
shall come the Kingdom which is in Heaven?' Jesus saith:
'The birds of the air and, of the beasts, whatsoever is
under the earth or upon the earth, and the fishes of the sea;
these are they which draw you. And the Kingdom of Heaven
is within you; and whosoever shall know himself shall find it.
And when ye have found it, ye shall know that ye are sons and
heirs of the almighty Father, and ye shall know that ye are in
God and God in you. And ye are the city of God.'

Critics differ widely as to the meaning to be attached to the participle ἕλκοντες (l. 10), and this disagreement together with the mutilation of the Saying and the absence of any general parallel to the whole, has given rise to a large number of reconstructions.

The renderings of ἕλκοντες may be grouped as follows: (1) GH[1] and Swete[2] understand 'attract' or 'influence'; (2) Taylor[3] takes the word in its literal and physical sense, 'pull' or 'draw'; (3) Bartlet[4] would interpret it 'persecute'; (4) Deissmann renders 'drag' (*sc.* before the judgement-seat). These views can be considered only briefly. Taylor's rendering must be rejected on the ground of the extreme *naïveté* it assumes on the part of the author of this Saying. That the birds of the air might be said to draw us up to Heaven, is perhaps admissible as a poetic

figure and not without a classical echo; but to claim that the beasts ' on the earth and under the earth ' also perform this service, borders on the ludicrous, while the admission of the fishes of the sea to the same privilege is surely intolerable[5]. Bartlet's reconstruction fails on the grounds given by GH, that authority over brute-creation hardly justifies the command 'fear not them who persecute you.' And it should be noticed that the parallel advanced by Bartlet from *Barnab.* VI 12 and 18 attributes this authority to mankind in general (following *Genesis* i 26). Deissmann's restoration[6] yields to none in ingenuity; but is it likely that unbelievers would be represented as making such a taunt? Surely the whole course of early Christian history shows that those who 'dragged Christians before the judgement-seats' failed to

[1] *Ox. Pap.* IV p. 7.   [2] *Expos. Times* XV 491.   [3] *Oxyrh. Sayings* pp. 9–10.
[4] In *Ox. Pap.* l.c.
[5] In *J.T.S.* VII p. 548, however, Dr Taylor compares Philo *de Praem. et Poen.*
(M. ii 415, 421) to the effect that by contemplation of the world and its order men
may rise up as on a sort of heavenly ladder to the thought of God.
[6] *Beilage zur Allgemeinen Zeitung* (1904) S. 117.

understand this very point that 'the Kingdom was in Heaven.' Moreover, the reconstruction of ll. 11–14 has a strange sound and makes but a lefthanded reply to the supposed taunt of the persecutors.

Bruston[1] fails to see any connection between birds, beasts and fishes and the Kingdom, but finds a double opposition (1) between birds and fishes, (2) between the Kingdom and those who draw us to the earth. But Matthew (as we shall see) gives a key to the connection between birds and the Kingdom, and *Psalm* viii, with many other passages[2], shows that birds, beasts and fishes are conventionally representative of the whole lower animate creation.

The sense in which GH and Swete understand ἕλκοντες is surely the right one, being supported, as the latter points out, by Clement (*Strom.* VII 2 § 9) who speaks of men as τῷ ἁγίῳ πνεύματι ἑλκόμενοι[3]: the discoverers also compare the use of ἑλκύειν in *John* vi 44 ; xii 32. Taking ἕλκοντες in some such sense, GH base their restoration ' on the close parallelism which we have supposed to exist between l. 15 -τες ὑμᾶς καὶ ἡ βασιλεία τῶν οὐρανῶν and l. 10 οἱ ἕλκοντες ἡμᾶς followed in l. 11 by ἡ βασιλεία ἐν οὐρανῷ.' Such a view, implying as it does that the Saying was in the form of question and answer, alone adequately explains the fragments of the text. The restoration ἕλκον]τες (ll. 14–15) is, of course, inevitable.

The restoration printed in our text rests upon two considerations to which perhaps too little impor-

tance has been attached. (1) In l. 10 the papyrus has ἡμᾶς and in l. 15 ὑμᾶς : the change may, as GH point out, be no more than an error which is very common in papyri ; yet a restoration which can retain the MS. reading has at least a slight advantage. (2) In l. 15 [οἱ ἕλκον]τες ὑμᾶς is separated from ἡ βασιλεία by καί: does this not force us to conclude that the parallel οἱ ἕλκοντες ἡμᾶς also was followed by καί, or, in other words, must we not the question have been a double one[4]? If this be so, the restorations hitherto put forward must be profoundly modified ; and it remains to give further grounds for the reconstruction here put forward. If the ἡμᾶς... ὑμᾶς of the papyrus is right, the question must have been put to Jesus by a second person (just as Saying V consists of a series of questions followed by an answer) : it cannot well be a rhetorical or echoed question as GH regard it, and it is most unlikely that Jesus would have included himself among those who are ' drawn' by the birds, beasts and fishes. In l. 9 the surviving λέγει Ἰ[... naturally suggests the familiar λέγει Ἰησοῦς ; but this is not inevitable, and I have conjectured λέγει Ἰούδας introducing the *question* (cp. *John* xiv 22, quoted below), and have filled out the otherwise difficult lacuna in l. 11 with the formula λέγει Ἰησοῦς which introduces the *answer*: why Judas has been selected as the interrogator will become clear later. If, again, the answer is in two parts, connected by καί, it is highly probable that the question also was similarly

[1] *Fragm. d'un anc. recueil de Paroles de Jésus* p. 114.
[2] *E.g.* Hesiod, *W. and D.* 277 ; *Job* xii 7, 8.
[3] Mr Badham cites further Clement *Strom.* VI 6 τοὺς μὲν γὰρ προτρέπει ὁ Κύριος· τοῖς δὲ ἤδη ἐγχειρήσασι καὶ χεῖρα ὀρέγει καὶ ἀνέλκει. *Id.* V 12 ἡ ἰσχὺς τοῦ Λόγου...πάντα τὸν καταδοξάμενον καὶ ἐντὸς ἑαυτοῦ πρὸς ἑαυτὴν ἕλκει.
[4] Dr Taylor (*J.T.S.* VII p. 548) regards καί as 'editorial': in view of the apparent parallelism between question and answer, this explanation cannot, I think, be maintained.

divided. Leaving on one side, then, the first part of the question 'Who are they who draw us?' with its answer 'These are they who draw you,' we must ask what was the second question which is answered by 'The Kingdom of Heaven is within you.' Now this answer is familiar enough. *Luke* xvii 20 has: ἐπερωτηθεὶς δὲ ὑπὸ τῶν Φαρισαίων πότε ἔρχεται ἡ βασιλεία τοῦ θεοῦ, ἀπεκρίθη αὐτοῖς καὶ εἶπεν· οὐκ ἔρχεται ἡ βασιλεία τοῦ θεοῦ μετὰ παρατηρήσεως...ἰδοὺ γάρ, ἡ βασιλεία τοῦ θεοῦ ἐντὸς ὑμῶν ἐστίν. Since Luke, then, gives the reply contained in our Saying as the answer to a definite question, and since we have reason to believe that our Saying contained a *double* question, is it not at least highly probable that the second part of the question which we are seeking to recover, was similar to the question answered in *Luke* by the remarkable saying 'The Kingdom of Heaven is within you'? I have therefore restored 'And when shall come (*or* cometh) the Kingdom which is in Heaven[1]?'

I have supposed that Judas ('not Iscariot') is the interrogator. Luke, indeed, makes the Saying 'The Kingdom of Heaven is within you' part of the reply to the Pharisees; but this is not likely to be historically true, inasmuch as the Pharisees are normally represented to us as the last people of whom it could be said that the Kingdom was within them. Possibly Luke had before him some notice of a question of the Pharisees, 'When is this Kingdom to appear?' and the detached *logos* ἡ β. ἐντὸς ὑμῶν, and uncritically welded the two together.

Judas, however, appears in *John* xiv 22 with a closely parallel question: λέγει αὐτῷ 'Ιούδας...κύριε, τί γέγονεν ὅτι ἡμῖν μέλλεις ἐμφανίζειν σεαυτὸν καὶ οὐχὶ τῷ κόσμῳ; where is latent the same contrast between a material and spiritual view of the Kingdom as in the present Saying. Hippolytus[2] also has preserved a notice of a question·asked by Judas (Iscariot?) concerning the Kingdom: τοῦ οὖν κυρίου διηγουμένου περὶ τῆς μελλούσης τῶν ἁγίων βασιλείας... καταπλαγεὶς ὁ 'Ιούδας...ἔφη· καὶ τίς ἄρα ὄψεται ταῦτα; We might almost suppose that the name of Judas became traditionally associated with a certain type of question, though possibly the two owners of that name were not always clearly distinguished.

We may now turn back to the remarkable reference to the birds, the beasts and the fishes. These, as we have seen, are representative of lower animate creation; but what is meant by saying that these 'draw' or 'influence' us? The answer is to be found, as Dr Taylor has shown[3], in *Matth.* vi 26-30, where the fowls of the air and the lilies of the field[4] are represented as drawing us, if we will but heed the lesson they teach, by their example of faith in providence[5]. Dr Taylor further compares *Job* xii 7-8 ἀλλὰ δὴ ἐρώτησον τετράποδα ἐάν σοι εἴπωσι, πετεινὰ δὲ οὐρανοῦ ἐάν σοι ἀπαγγείλωσιν· ἐκδιήγησαι γῇ ἐάν σοι φράσῃ, καὶ ἐξηγήσονταί σοι οἱ ἰχθύες τῆς θαλάσσης, a passage which alike in its main thought and in its phraseology lies so closely parallel to our Saying as to make almost inevitable the conclusion that the com-

---

[1] For another setting of this question cf. 2 *Clem.* XII 2.
[2] *Comm. in Dan.* IV 60 (=Preuschen *Antileg.* p. 29 no. 23 b).
[3] *Oxyrh. Sayings* p. 11.
[4] Cp. also *Luke* xii 24 ff.
[5] Cp. *Hymns Anc. and Mod.* 276, especially the last stanza.

piler of the Saying elaborated the essential idea of Matthew or Luke[1] on a model derived from the Old Testament.

In this connection it will be well to consider the relation between our Saying and Luke in regard to the *logos* ἡ βασιλεία τῶν οὐρανῶν ἐντὸς ὑμῶν ἐστιν. GH, indeed, incline to see connection between the Saying and the Gospel of Thomas, quoting Hippolytus *Refut.* v 7 οὐ μόνον δ' αὐτῶν ἐπιμαρτυρεῖν φασὶ τῷ λόγῳ τὰ Ἀσσυρίων μυστήρια, ἀλλὰ καὶ Φρυγῶν περὶ τὴν τῶν γεγονότων καὶ γινομένων καὶ ἐσομένων ἔτι μακαρίαν κρυβομένην ὁμοῦ καὶ φανερουμένην φύσιν ἥνπερ φασὶ τὴν ἐντὸς ἀνθρώπου βασιλείαν οὐρανῶν ζητουμένην, περὶ ἧς διαρρήδην ἐν τῷ κατὰ Θωμᾶν ἐπιγραφομένῳ εὐαγγελίῳ παραδιδόασι λέγοντες οὕτως· ἐμὲ ὁ ζητῶν εὑρήσει ἐν παιδίοις ἀπὸ ἐτῶν ἑπτά· ἐκεῖ γὰρ ἐν τῷ τεσσαρεσκαιδεκάτῳ αἰῶνι κρυβόμενος φανεροῦμαι. But surely this passage does not state or imply that the *logos* was found also in the *Gospel of Thomas*: it seems clear that the Naassenes urged in defence of their doctrine, 'The Happy Nature, in which we believe, is the same as your canonical doctrine of the Kingdom of Heaven within a man, though its nature is more explicitly revealed in a *logos* in our own *Gospel of Thomas*.' The *logos*, then, is common to Luke and our Saying alone: are we to suppose that the evangelist and the logographer derived it from the same source or parallel sources, or that one is indebted to the other? Circumstantial evidence makes it probable, if not certain, that the Saying is indebted to the Gospel; for (1) we have already seen good reason to believe that the first part is composite and owes one of

its elements to the first Gospel ; (2) if the second part of the Saying is genuine and not a later addition, its mystical and quasi-philosophical character demands a post-synoptic date; (3) the other Sayings generally betray dependence upon one or more of the Synoptics, and analogy therefore is in favour of a similar dependence here.

The second part of the Saying is less compact than the first, and restoration is consequently more hazardous. No detailed criticism of the suggestions hitherto published, therefore, is likely to serve any good purpose : it will be sufficient to remark on the new supplements given in the text as they occur. The restoration of GH in l. 16 is certainly right, and that of Heinrici in l. 17 almost equally so. In l. 18 I have substituted κληρονόμοι (for which compare *Luke* x 25 but especially *Romans* viii 14, 16–17 ὅσοι γὰρ πνεύματι θεοῦ ἄγονται, οὗτοί εἰσιν υἱοὶ θεοῦ...αὐτὸ τὸ πνεῦμα συμμαρτυρεῖ...ὅτι ἐσμὲν τέκνα θεοῦ· εἰ δὲ τέκνα, καὶ κληρονόμοι· κληρονόμοι μὲν θεοῦ, συγκληρονόμοι δὲ Χριστοῦ) for θυγατέρες (Swete, Taylor). In l.19 the discoverers' παντοκράτορος[2] may well be right, though the epithet is a matter of minor importance. Lines 20–21 are decidedly difficult : in the former only the suggestion of Heinrici ἐν τῷ πατρὶ ὑμῶν seems plausible. Following his suggestion, I had once thought of ἐν ἐμοὶ ὄντας κἀμὲ ἐν ὑμῖν (cf. *John* vi 56 ; xiv 20 ; xv 5) ; but this is a little too long ; and I therefore read ἐν θ(ε)ῷ ὄντας καὶ θ(εὸ)ν ἐν ὑμῖν, and compare 1 *John* iv 13 ἐν τούτῳ γινώσκομεν ὅτι ἐν αὐτῷ μένομεν καὶ αὐτὸς ἐν ἡμῖν ὅτι ἐκ τοῦ πνεύματος αὐτοῦ δέδωκεν ἡμῖν. In the latter Blass' supplement ἡ πτό[λις[3] alone seems pos-

---

[1] The common phrase τὰ πετεινὰ τοῦ οὐρανοῦ makes it likely that Matthew rather than Luke, who has κόρακες, was in the compiler's mind.
[2] Cp. 2 *Cor.* vi 18. [3] Cp. *Matth.* v 14.

14

SAYINGS OF JESUS

sible; and though the change of subject is abrupt, this is not necessarily an objection. I have adopted Prof. Bethune Baker's suggestion (privately communicated) that θ(εο)ῦ should be added.

The second part of the Saying in its abstract and philosophical character stands in strong contrast against the first. While the earlier portion is redolent of the countryside, the latter sounds like an echo from Alexandria[1] or some similar centre, and it seems at least possible that this part of the Saying is an addition to the less artificial first half.

Whether the second part is an amplification or no, there seems good ground for believing that the first part at least is an extract from a larger context. Whether the Saying began 'Ye ask who are they who draw us' (or the like), or '[Judas] saith: Who, then, are they who draw us?' it must have been preceded by some enigmatic statement which provoked the question (whether real or assumed), by some such statement as 'Ye shall be drawn unto the Kingdom.' If this be granted, the passage to which our Saying belonged was of the same type as the citation in 2 Clement v discussed in the Commentary on Saying IV, and this citation, as I have there tried to show, must come from the *Gospel according to the Hebrews.* In itself this attribution is obviously precarious; but the Saying seems to show certain tendencies which may in some

degree strengthen it: (1) there is a *naïve* unconventionality in the statement that birds, beasts and fishes 'draw' us which is generally similar to the spirit of the well-known fragment[2] from the *Gospel according to the Hebrews,* ἄρτι ἔλαβέ με ἡ μήτηρ μου τὸ ἅγιον πνεῦμα ἐν μιᾷ τῶν τριχῶν μου καὶ ἀπήνεγκέ με εἰς τὸ ὄρος τὸ μέγα Θαβώρ: both passages, moreover, seem to be adaptations from ancient Hebrew literature[3]. (2) The metaphysical and theological character of the second part of the Saying (apart from restorations) on the one hand is Johannine—and as we have seen in the Introduction the *Gospel according to the Hebrews* shows a distinct though minor Johannine element—, and on the other lies parallel to Saying I, which is attributed by Clement of Alexandria to the same Gospel.

The argument of the Saying as a whole seems to be that men can be greatly influenced towards the Kingdom by the example of faith and trust shown by the lower creation; for the Kingdom is not a material one: it is latent in man and consists in his capacities for faith, trust, and the like. When a man becomes conscious of these and develops them (knows himself)— a process in which the example of the birds of the air and other creatures exercises a powerful influence—, he has found the Kingdom, and realizes all that this implies, sonship with God and unity with God.

---

[1] Cp. Clement of Alexandria *Paedag.* III 1 (quoted by Badham in *Ox. Pap.* IV 7) ἦν ἄρα, ὡς ἔοικε, πάντων μέγιστον μαθημάτων τὸ γνῶναι αὑτόν· ἑαυτὸν γάρ τις ἐὰν γνῷ, θεὸν εἴσεται.
[2] Orig. *Comm. in Ioh.* ii 12 87.
[3] *Job* xii 7–8; *Ezech.* viii 3.

SAYING III

λέγει Ἰη(σοῦ)ς·
οὐκ ἀποκνήσει ἄνθ[ρωπος τὴν ὁδὸν εὑ-]
ρῶν ἐπερωτῆσαι πά[ντα......διαι-]
ρῶν περὶ τοῦ τόπου τῆ[ς καθέδρας; εὑρή-]
σετε ὅτι πολλοὶ ἔσονται π[ρῶτοι ἔσχατοι, καὶ] 25
οἱ ἔσχατοι πρῶτοι· καὶ [ζωὴν κληρονομήσου-]
σιν.

22–27. ἄνθρωπος κληθεὶς σώφρων ἐ. πάντως ἕνα τῶν κλητόρων π. τ. τ. τῆς δοχῆς ποῦ ἀνακλιθήσεται ὅ. π. ἔ. πρῶτοι ἔσχατοι καὶ οἱ ἔ. πρῶτοι καὶ δόξαν εὑρήσουσιν, Deissmann.

οὐκ ἀποκνήσει ἄνθρωπος (ὢν) τῶν ἐντιμοτέρων ἐπερωτῆσαι παρὰ τοῦ δείπνου ἀπορῶν περὶ τοῦ τόπου τῆς κλισίας ποῦ κλιθήσεται· ὅτι π. ἔ. πρῶτοι ἔσχατοι καὶ οἱ ἔ. π. καὶ φανεροὶ ἀποβαίνουσιν, Wessely.

ἄνθρωπος περὶ τῶν καιρῶν ἐ. παρρησιαζόμενος ληρῶν περὶ τοῦ τ. τῆς δόξης· ὑμεῖς δὲ σιωπήσετε (κτλ.) καὶ ὀλίγοι εὑρήσουσιν, Swete.

ἄνθρωπος πλήρης ἡμερῶν ἐ. παρὰ τῶν πρεσβυτέρων περὶ τ. τ. τῆς μονῆς αὐτοῦ. ἀλλ' εὑρήσετε (κτλ.) καὶ ὀλίγοι κλητοί εἰσιν, Taylor.

22 ff. ἄνθρωπος νέος καὶ σώφρων ἐ. παρὰ τῶν πρεσβυτέρων π. τ. τ. τῆς ἀναπαύσεως· καὶ γνώσετε ὅ. π. ἔ. (κτλ.) καὶ ὡς ὁ ἥλιος ἐκλάμψουσιν, Bruston.

22. περὶ τῶν πατέρων, Bartlet.   23. παρρησίᾳ καὶ ἱστορῶν, Bartlet.
ΕΠΕΡΩΤΗϹΕ, P (corr. GH).   24. τῆς βασιλείας εἰδήσετε, GH.
25. ὅτι, suprascript in P.   26. ζωὴν αἰώνιον ἕξουσιν, GH.

Jesus saith:
Shall a man who has found the way not fear to ask...determining all things concerning the place of his seat? Ye shall find that many first shall be last, and the last first, and they shall inherit eternal life.

The discoverers offer no restoration for the main part of this Saying, and those of Swete, Deissmann, Taylor and Bruston are, on general grounds, not satisfactory. Mr Badham has suggested comparison with *Apoc. Petr.* λέγει ἡμῖν ὁ κύριος·

οὗτός ἐστιν ὁ τόπος τῶν ἀρχερων†
ὑμῶν τῶν δικαίων ἀνθρώπων ; but no reconstruction on this basis seems possible.
I have ventured to follow what seems to be another possible line of restoration. Here, as elsewhere in

16   SAYINGS OF JESUS

the Sayings, the Synoptics seem to give the safest clue, and the latter part of this Saying is obviously very close to the Synoptic Gospels. *Matth.* xix–xx has a series of incidents which are likely to help us. First (xix 27 ff.) we have τότε ἀποκριθεὶς ὁ Πέτρος εἶπεν αὐτῷ· Ἰδοὺ ἡμεῖς ἀφήκαμεν πάντα...τί ἄρα ἔσται ἡμῖν ; εἶπεν ὁ Ἰησοῦς ... καθίσεσθε καὶ ὑμεῖς ἐπὶ δώδεκα θρόνους...πολλοὶ δὲ ἔσονται πρῶτοι ἔσχατοι κτλ. Then follows the Parable of the Labourers in the Vineyard (xx 1–16), ending like the preceding incident and the present Saying. Thirdly we have the episode of the ‘mother of Zebedee's children’ who asks precedence for her two sons (xx 20–24). Lastly Jesus himself utters a warning to those who seek the first place. These passages form a group which might be headed ‘On seeking Precedence,’ and the warning ‘the first shall be last’ surely links the whole with our Saying. It is highly probable, then, that the Saying also deals with the matter of seeking precedence in the Kingdom ; and this probability is increased by the use of τόπος, a word which in *Luke* xiv 9–10 means ‘place’ (the ‘room’ of A.V.) with a definite connotation of precedence[1].

In consequence, the restoration of τῆς καθέδρας in l. 24 seems almost inevitable—οὐκ ἀποκνήσει should then be treated as an indignant question ; and we may here assume that the lacuna after ἄνθρωπος was once occupied by words which gave reason why a man

should be ashamed to ask of such matters. I have therefore restored τὴν ὁδὸν εὑρών[2]. The general sense of the Saying would then be : ‘a man who has found the one great and essential thing (the Way) ought to be ashamed to haggle about his precedence over others.’

There remains the lacuna in l. 23 which I cannot fill with any confidence. The missing words may possibly have been explanatory of ἐπερωτῆσαι, and I have accordingly suggested πά[ντα... διαι]ρῶν[3], ‘determining (or trying to determine) all things concerning the place,’ etc. The completion of l. 26 is a matter of only secondary importance. GH suggest ζωὴν αἰώνιον ἕξουσιν[4], which is adequate ; but *Matth.* xix 29 may be thought to favour ζωὴν κληρονομήσουσιν.

The Saying—however we restore it—is a remarkable instance of that salient characteristic of the Oxyrhynchus collection as a whole—the mixture of elements at once parallel to and divergent from the Synoptics. For while the first part of the Saying has nothing exactly similar in the Synoptics, it nevertheless seems related to a clearly marked group of episodes in the Gospels. On the other hand the second part of the Saying corresponds exactly with the Synoptic version, and as compared with *Mark* x 31 this correspondence is exact (Mark, indeed, inserts δέ after πολλοί, but this is due to his different context) : *Matth.* xix 30 differs only in the omission of οἱ before the second ἔσχατοι[5]. The

[1] Note that almost immediately above (xiii 29–30) Luke says ‘they shall come from the east and from the west...and shall sit down (ἀνακλιθήσονται) in the kingdom of God. And lo, there are last which shall be first,’ etc. (This after speaking of the rejection of the self-righteous.)
[2] Cp. 1 *Clement* xxxvi αὕτη ἡ ὁδός...ἐν ᾗ εὕρομεν τὸ σωτήριον ἡμῶν Ἰησοῦν Χριστόν ; *John* xiv 4 καὶ ὅπου ἐγὼ ὑπάγω οἴδατε τὴν ὁδόν.
[3] For this use of διαιρεῖν cp. Aristotle *Phys.* VI 9 2.
[4] Cp. *John* iii 16, 36 ; v 24.
[5] *Luke's* εἰσὶν ἔσχατοι οἳ ἔσονται πρῶτοι κτλ. (xiv 30) is obviously remote from the present question.

Synoptics and the Saying are indeed so close that it is incredible that the two are independent, and the evidence reviewed in the Introduction goes to show that it is the writer of the Saying who is the borrower. The points of difference between the versions of Matthew and Mark are, however, so slight that it is impossible to say with certainty whether the author of the Saying borrowed from the first or the second : only we may be sure that he borrowed from one of them.

The abrupt rebuke conveyed in the first part of the Saying reproving as it surely does the tendency to seek for precedence, can hardly be anything but an extract : it must have formed part, not of any general exhortation, but of a reply to some request. It is, indeed, only intelligible to one who can reconstruct the context. If conjecture is permissible, we might regard the Saying as coming from a lost version of the incident of the Sons of Zebedee.

SAYING IV

λέγει Ἰη(σοῦ)ς· [πᾶν τὸ μὴ ἔμπροσ-]
θεν τῆς ὄψεώς σου, καὶ [τὸ κεκαλυμμένον]
ἀπό σου ἀποκαλυφ⟨θ⟩ήσετ[αί σοι· οὐ γάρ ἐσ-]
τιν κρυπτὸν ὃ οὐ φανε[ρὸν γενήσεται,]   30
καὶ τεθαμμένον ὃ ο[ὐκ ἐγερθήσεται].

28. τὸ κεκρυμμένον, *GH*.   29. ·ΑΠΟΚΑΛΥΦΗCΕΤΑΙ, *P*, *Wessely*[1] (corr. *GH*).   30. φαίνῃ τοῖς...οὐρανίοις or ὃ οὐ φύσις φανερώσει ποτέ *Bruston*.   31. ΘΕΘΑΜΜΕΝΟΝ, *P* (corr. *GH*) : οὐ γνωσθήσεται *GH* (alternative reading) : οὐκ ἐξορύξεται, *Bartlet* : οὐ φανερὸν ᾖ αὐτοῖς or οὐκ ἐξορύξει, *Bruston*.

Jesus saith :
Every thing that is not before thine eyes,
And that which is hidden from thee, shall be revealed unto thee ;
For there is nothing hid that shall not become manifest,
And buried that shall not be raised up.

The restoration of this Saying does not admit of much controversy : the second half of l. 30 and of l. 31 do indeed admit of different supplements ; but these do not affect the general structure and

meaning of the whole. As far as I know, Bruston alone has disturbed this critical calm. In l. 30 he objects[2] to the discoverers' φανε[ρόν and thinks that φίνῃ (= φαίνῃ) or φύσις[3] should be read.

---

[1] Comparing the analogous form of the aorist passive participle ἀποκαλυφείσης: see *Karanis et Sknopaiu Nesos* in *Mém. Acad. de Vienne* XLVII p. 6.
[2] *Fragm. d'un anc. recueil de Paroles de Jésus*, p. 17.   [3] *Ib.* p. 34.

The first half of this Saying is new, though *John* xiii 7 ὃ ἐγὼ ποιῶ σὺ οὐκ οἶδας ἄρτι, γνώσῃ δὲ μετὰ ταῦτα affords a parallel in the most general sense.

The latter half has parallels in all three Synoptics, Luke giving two versions of the Saying. These passages may be divided into two groups, as follows :

I (a) *Mark* iv 22 οὐ γάρ ἐστί τι κρυπτὸν ἐὰν μὴ ἵνα φανερωθῇ, οὐδὲ ἐγένετο ἀπόκρυφον ἀλλ᾽ ἵνα εἰς φανερὸν ἔλθῃ.

   (b) *Luke* viii 17 οὐ γάρ ἐστι κρυπτὸν ὃ οὐ φανερὸν γενήσεται, οὐδὲ ἀπόκρυφον ὃ οὐ μὴ γνωσθῇ καὶ εἰς φανερὸν ἔλθῃ.

II (a) *Matth.* x 26 οὐδὲν γάρ ἐστι κεκαλυμμένον ὃ οὐκ ἀποκαλυφθήσεται καὶ κρυπτὸν ὃ οὐ γνωσθή-σεται.

   (b) *Luke* xii 2 οὐδὲν δὲ συγ-κεκαλυμμένον ἐστὶν ὃ οὐκ ἀποκαλυφθήσεται καὶ κρυπτὸν ὃ οὐ γνωσθή-σεται.

In the first of these groups, where Luke is clearly dependent upon Mark, the Saying occurs in a series of disconnected logia and is therefore without context ; but in the second we find it in the Charge to the Twelve (*Matth.* x 5 ff.), or to the Seventy (*Luke* x 1 ff.), though the third evangelist defers some of the most characteris-tic matter—including the parallel to the present Saying—to chapter xii. Our authorities for the Saying in its two-fold form are, then, Mark (for Group I) and Q (for Group II). Whether the latter owes its context to the ingenuity of an editor or no, is a matter which need not be dis-cussed here : the question before us is the relationship of Saying IV to this double tradition. Grenfell and Hunt consider it to agree with Matthew and Luke (Group II)

in general arrangement, but with Mark in the language of the first clause of the second half. Else-where—in the *Logia* of 1897 as in the Sayings of 1903—the influence of Mark is very slight, if indeed it exists, while that of Matthew and Luke is strongly marked. Now the first clause of the second half of Saying IV coincides word for word with the Lucan parallel in Group I, and it therefore seems likely that Mark should be left out of the matter altogether. On the other hand the relationship be-tween the Saying and Group II seems to extend beyond arrange-ment. ἀποκαλυφθήσεται is peculiar to the Q version—a fact which suggests that another Q word, κεκαλυμμένον, should be supplied instead of the discoverers' κεκρυμμέ-νον. It may, then, be claimed that the Saying is dependent partly upon the Q tradition, and partly upon the Lucan version of Mark's tradition.

This, together with the novel first and fourth clauses, calls for explanation. The Saying would seem to have grown in the follow-ing way : the final clause either grew up naturally in post-apostolic days, or (as is more likely in view of the dependence of the third clause upon Luke viii) was de-liberately substituted for the final clause in the version of Group I. Then, it appears, this revised Say-ing was contaminated with the Group II version, its first clause superseding the second clause of Group II, which it closely resem-bles. In consequence the first clause of Group II was left out of the parallelistic scheme, but was retained by prefixing a totally new first clause. It is significant that this clause contains the Johan-nine word ὄψις.

Is Saying IV an extract ? If so, we must—in view of its relation-ship to Group II—assign it to a version of the Charge to the Apostles (or to the Seventy), though the remarkable final clause indicates that the *particular* connection must have been other than Synoptic. The discoverers, indeed, held that the Prologue claimed S. Thomas as the authority for the Sayings, and that it is therefore inconceivable that the Collection is a series of excerpts from well-known Gospels. In the notes on the Prologue I have shown reason for believing that the mention of Thomas is there only casual, and that he was not claimed by the Editor as the source from which the Oxyrhynchus Sayings were derived. Consequently, there is no initial objection to the theory that the Sayings are extracts.

Does our Saying then show signs of extraction from a context? The use of the second person singular is remarkable: it gives the Saying a precision and directness which an isolated *logion* would hardly be likely to preserve. It is used, indeed, in discourses as an oratorical device to secure vividness[1], but this explanation does not seem to meet the present case. Surely Saying IV is addressed to an individual, and the striking character of the final clause may be taken as lending support to this conclusion, since the departure from the Synoptic version may well be due to use in a more specialized context—a context in which such a version would be particularly appropriate.

This context may perhaps be recoverable. We have seen that the Saying in its Synoptic setting is part of the great missionary Charge, but we must here note that neither in the version of Matthew nor in that of Luke is

any *individual* specially prominent. Yet our Saying is, apparently, addressed to an individual. Now the author of the *Second Epistle of Clement*[2] has an interesting fragment of a version of the Charge which is related to the Synoptic versions, but diverges markedly from them. In this, the individual, St Peter, is introduced. The passage is as follows : λέγει γὰρ ὁ κύριος· ἔσεσθε ὡς ἀρνία ἐν μέσῳ λύκων. ἀποκριθεὶς δὲ ὁ Πέτρος αὐτῷ λέγει· ἐὰν οὖν διασπαράξωσιν οἱ λύκοι τὰ ἀρνία; εἶπεν ὁ Ἰησοῦς τῷ Πέτρῳ· μὴ φοβείσθωσαν τὰ ἀρνία τοὺς λύκους μετὰ τὸ ἀποθανεῖν αὐτά καὶ ὑμεῖς μὴ φοβεῖσθε τοὺς ἀποκτείνοντας ὑμᾶς καὶ μηδὲν ὑμῖν δυναμένους ποιεῖν· ἀλλὰ φοβεῖσθε τὸν μετὰ τὸ ἀποθανεῖν ὑμᾶς ἔχοντα ἐξουσίαν ψυχῆς καὶ σώματος τοῦ βαλεῖν εἰς γέενναν πυρός. In this citation from an unnamed gospel the monologue is broken by an interlocutor—St Peter. May not our Saying well have been the reply to another question? I will venture to suggest what this question may have been. A very noteworthy deviation from the Synoptic version in the Clementine passage is the oxymoron ' those that kill you *and can do nothing to you.*' We shall see presently that the citation is highly rhetorical : for the present, is it not likely that the oxymoron is intended to evoke another question which might be restored as follows?—ἀποκριθεὶς δὲ ὁ Πέτρος λέγει· κύριε, πῶς λέγεις τοὺς ἀποκτείνοντας ἡμᾶς μηδὲν ἡμῖν δύνασθαι ποιεῖν; The reply to such a question might well be in the form of our Saying : ' you do not understand this now[3], but later it will become clear ; for that which is hidden shall be revealed, and that which has been buried shall

---

[1] *Matth.* vii 3, though the Saying may well be one which has lost its real context (in some incident) and been worked up here for convenience.
[2] § 5.   [3] Cp. *John* xiii 7.

20 SAYINGS OF JESUS

be raised up.' The remarkable fourth clause of our Saying becomes very apt in such a context.

If, then, the Saying is a fragment from the gospel used by pseudo-Clement, can we discover which of the many rejected gospels this was? Lightfoot and Harnack have, indeed, consigned all pseudo-Clement's citations to the Egyptian Gospel, chiefly because one of them [1] appears to be a part of the dialogue with Salome cited by Clement of Alexandria from that Gospel. The citation in question may indeed be from the *Gospel according to the Egyptians*; but we now know that that document was not the only record of the material contained in that dialogue [2]. And if it were certain that pseudo-Clement used this Gospel once, the fact would not prove that he used no other. Indeed, it would be hard to imagine a more complete contrast than that which exists between the remaining Clementine citations on the one hand, and the Salome dialogue as preserved by the Alexandrian Clement on the other: the former are Synoptic in character and of the type of the First and Third Gospels, while what little we actually know of the Egyptian Gospel [3] indicates that that document was of a very different character. Now the Clementine fragment of the missionary Charge shows a peculiar rhetorical structure. It commences with an abrupt statement 'Ye shall be as lambs in the midst of wolves.' In its brevity and obvious incompleteness this is certainly designed to lead on to the question which follows—a ques-

tion, however, which is not particularly forcible. This put, the monologue continues by way of formal reply. The arrangement—which is not likely to have any historical foundation — seems intended to relieve the monologue by introducing a kind of dramatic variety. Possibly, then, this rhetorical structure will serve as a clue to the source of the Clementine citation, and so—if the connection between this and the Oxyrhynchus Saying be admitted—to that of our Saying. Happily a passage which shows exactly the same structure is extant. Jerome [4] cites the following passage from the *Gospel according to the Hebrews*: "'Si peccaverit,' inquit, 'frater tuus in verbo et satis tibi fecerit, septies in die suscipe eum.' Dixit illi Simon discipulus eius: 'Septies in die?' Respondit dominus et dixit ei: 'Etiam ego dico tibi usque septuagies septies.'" Here as in the Clementine citation we have first an abrupt statement, then the mechanical question of the interlocutor, and lastly the remainder of the canonical Saying, here made into a response [5].

Stylistic considerations at least do not oppose the ascription of the Oxyrhynchus Saying to the *Gospel according to the Hebrews*. At the outset of these notes we saw that the Saying depends upon Matthew and Luke, and later we recalled that pseudo-Clement's citations in general have the same tendency. The fragment of the missionary Charge is certainly Matthaean in the connected form it gives to that address, but the influence of the Third Gospel is perhaps to be

---

[1] Preuschen *Antilegomena* p. 2 f.
[2] The Saying about "trampling on the Garment of Shame" occurs in the Oxyrhynchus Gospel fragment (*Ox. Pap.* IV no. 655).
[3] Cp. Batiffol *Rév. Bibl.* 1897 pp. 513–15.
[4] *C. Pelag.* III 2 (Preuschen *Antilegomena* p. 6 no. 10 a).
[5] There is not the least doubt that such dramatic presentations of Sayings are later than their canonical versions, though Handmann (*das Hebr. Evang.* p. 87) thinks Jerome's citation is earlier than its parallel in Matthew and Luke.

seen in the use of ἀρνία¹. In Jerome's citation this double influence is more clearly marked, the words *in die* depending on *Luke* xvii 4, while *septuagies septies* is a phrase borrowed from Matthew (xviii 21–22)². The whole question both of the derivation of the Oxyrhynchus Sayings from the *Gospel according to the Hebrews* and of the dependence of that Gospel upon Matthew and Luke has been considered in the Introduction.

It may be well to sum up by way of conclusion the various heads of the theory for which I have been arguing. (1) The Saying in its use of the second person singular is, so far, extra-Synoptic, and a parallel to this feature can be found only in the fragment of the missionary Charge preserved by pseudo-Clement. (2) This citation is remarkable in style, and in this regard is identical with a frag-

ment known to belong to the *Gospel according to the Hebrews*. (3) The Saying on the one part, and the apocryphal excerpts with which we are here concerned on the other, have an identical relation to the Synoptics.

Alternatively, this Saying might be thought to be an explanation substituted by the Hebrews Evangelist for the rebuke to St Peter in the episode recorded in *Matth.* xvi 21–23 (=*Mark* viii 30–33). Following out this conjecture we may suppose that the passage in St Matthew was combined with its doublet *Matth.* xvii 22–23, where the first evangelist leaves an opening for questions, whereas *Luke* ix 45, *Mark* ix 32 state that the disciples did not understand the saying (καὶ ἦν παρακεκαλυμμένον ἀπ' αὐτῶν : *Luke* ix 45) and feared to ask for an explanation.

SAYING V

ἐξ]ετάζουσιν αὐτὸν ο[ἱ μαθηταὶ αὐτοῦ καὶ
λέ]γουσιν· πῶς νηστεύ[σομεν, καὶ πῶς προσ-
ευξό]μεθα καὶ πῶς [ἐλεημοσύνην ποιήσομεν, κ]αὶ τί παρατηρήσ[ομεν τῶν παραδο- 35
θέντω]ν; λέγει Ἰησ(οῦ)ς· [οὐκ ἔσεσθε ὡς οἱ
ὑποκρ]ιταί· μὴ ποιεῖτ[ε ταῦτα φανερῶς,
ἀλλὰ τ]ῆς ἀληθείας ἀν[τέχεσθε, καὶ ἡ δικαιοσύνη ὑμῶ]ν ἀ[π]οκεκρ[υμμένη ἔστω· λέγω γάρ· μα]κάρι[ός] ἐστιν [ὁ ταῦτα ποιῶν ἐν 40
κρυπτῷ, ὅτι ἐν φανερ]ῷ ἔστ[αι ὁ μισθὸς αὐτοῦ
παρὰ τῷ πατρὶ ὅς ἐστ]ιν [ἐν τοῖς οὐρανοῖς.

¹ Matthew (x 16) uses πρόβατα, Luke (x 3) ἄρνας.
² Cp. Adeney *Hibbert Journal* III 154. Jerome's fragment indeed uses the title dominus (κύριος), while Clement's fragment uses Ἰησοῦς. This however is no objection to my theory: Luke uses both Ἰησοῦς and κύριος (see x 1, 39–41 ; xi 39 ; xii 42; xiii 15 ; xvii 5).

33 ff. πῶς νηστεύσωμεν καὶ πῶς προσευξώμεθα καὶ πῶς ἐ. ποιήσωμεν καὶ
τί παρατηρησώμεθα τῶν τοιούτων; λ. Ἰ.· βλέπετε μὴ τὸν μισθὸν ἀπολεῖτε.
μὴ ποιεῖτε μηδὲν εἰ μὴ τὰ τῆς ἀληθείας· ἂν γὰρ ποιῆτε ταῦτα γνώσεσθε
μυστήριον ἀποκεκρυμμένον· λέγω ὑμῖν· μακάριός ἐστιν ὃς ἄν..., *Swete.*

33 ff. πῶς νηστεύσομεν καὶ πῶς ἀπολουσόμεθα καὶ πῶς προσευξόμεθα τὸν
κύριον καὶ τί παρατηρήσομεν· ἵνα ζωὴν κληρονομήσωμεν; λ. Ἰ. τοῖς
μαθηταῖς· ὡς ὑποκρειταὶ μὴ ποιεῖτε ὑμεῖς, ἀλλὰ ὡς οἱ υἱοὶ τῆς ἀληθείας
ἀναβλέπετε εἰς τὸν θεὸν ἀλλὰ οὐχ ἵνα ἀποκείσηται ὑμῖν μισθός. ὁ τοῦτο
ποιῶν μακάριός ἐστιν καὶ ἡ βασιλεία τῶν οὐρανῶν αὐτῷ ἐστίν, *Bruston.*

34 ff. καὶ πῶς ἐλεημοσύνην δώσομεν καὶ τί παρατηρησόμεθα καὶ ποιήσομεν; λ. Ἰ.· οὐκ ἔσεσθε ὡς οἱ ὑποκριταί· μὴ ποιεῖτε ὑμεῖς ψεῦδος ἀλλὰ τῆς
ἀληθείας ἀντέχεσθε. ἔστω δὲ ἡ ζωὴ ὑμῶν ἀποκεκρυμμένη ἀπὸ τοῦ κόσμου.
μακάριός ἐστιν..., *Taylor.*

35. παρατηρήσομεν ζητοῦντες τὴν βασιλείαν (*or* τὴν ζωήν), *Heinrici.*

35 ff. καὶ τί παρατηρήσομεν ἵνα ζωὴν ἔχωμεν; λ. Ἰ.· ὡς ποιοῦσιν οἱ
ὑποκριταὶ μὴ ποιεῖτε ὑμεῖς; τῇ γὰρ ὁδῷ τῆς ἀληθείας ἀνθίστανται, τὸν δὲ
μισθὸν τὸν ἀποκεκρυμμένον ἀθετοῦσιν· καὶ μακάριός ἐστιν ᾧ ὁ μισθὸς ἐν
οὐρανῷ ἐστίν..., *Barnes.*

37. ὑποκρ]ιταί, *Taylor*:]ειται, *P.*   39. τὸ μάννα τὸ κεκρυμμένον,
Lock.

His disciples examine him and say : How shall we fast,
and how shall we pray, and how shall we do alms, and what
shall we keep of the traditions? Jesus saith : Ye shall not be
as the hypocrites. Do not these things openly, but cleave to
the truth ; and let your righteousness be concealed. For I say :
Blessed is he that doeth these things in secret, for he shall be
rewarded openly by the Father who is in Heaven.

The condition of the Saying is
such as to discourage restoration,
and the discoverers have confined
themselves to the completion of
l. 32 and the filling of some of the
smaller lacunae. Here, as elsewhere in the Sayings, the only
hope for a plausible restoration lies
in following whatever clue the
canonical Gospels may offer.

Let us first consider the restoration of the question to which the
Saying proper is a reply. The
discoverers' supplement for l. 32

is inevitable : as they remark,
Φαρισαῖοι is not likely in view of
what follows, nor, it may be added,
would such a reading as οἱ μαθηταὶ
Ἰωάννου, since John had already
given definite teaching on both
fasting and prayer[1]. We pass on
then to the four questions put by
the disciples. The first alone is
adequately preserved, but the
second may be confidently restored as 'How shall we pray?'
both because the fragmentary reading of the papyrus seems to point

[1] *Luke* xi 1.

to this, and because fasting and prayer are continually linked together as two inseparable things. No word survives in the papyrus to indicate directly the subjects of the third and fourth questions, yet these also may be recovered if we can find and follow a Synoptic clue. Now in *Matth.* vi a series of subjects are discussed—(1) Almsgiving (*vv.* 2–4), (2) Prayer (*vv.* 5–15), (3) Fasting (*vv.* 16–18)—which furnish parallels to the first question. May we not then confidently conclude that the subject of the third question in our Saying was almsgiving[1]? If further parallel is needed to support the association of these three, reference may be made to the pseudo-Athanasian λόγος σωτηρίας πρὸς παρθένον § xii p. 46 (von der Goltz): ὅλον τὸν χρόνον τῆς ζωῆς σου ἐν νηστείαις καὶ προσευχαῖς καὶ ἐλεημοσύναις διατέλει. The restoration of the fourth question is less obvious: the supplements of Swete and Taylor seem too vague to be acceptable; indeed, they do not amount to a really distinct question such as is needed. On the other hand, Bruston's suggestion 'what shall we observe, that we may inherit eternal life?' is altogether too wide, since the disciples are obviously inquiring on particular points. The discoverers[2], however, threw out a suggestion which has been strangely neglected, 'How far, it was probably asked, are existing Jewish ordinances to be kept?' Now the verb παρατηρήσομεν[3] at once suggests comparison with *Mark* vii 9 καλῶς ἀθετεῖτε τὴν ἐντολὴν τοῦ θεοῦ

ἵνα τὴν παραδόσιν ὑμῶν τηρήσητε, and παραδοθέντων may be restored in our Saying. This explains the form of the question ('*what* shall we observe'): fasting, prayer and almsgiving are fundamental things, and the disciples need only ask *how* these are to be performed; but they would naturally ask *what* was to be kept and what rejected of the less authorised mass of Jewish ritual and ceremonial tradition[4]. But if (as seems to be the case) the first three questions are parallel to, and perhaps derived from, a part of the Sermon on the Mount, how are we to account for the association with them of the fourth question as we have restored it? That section of the Sermon on the Mount which precedes the teaching on prayer, fasting and almsgiving, is a series of corrections and amplifications of the Old Law, introduced by the formula ἠκούσατε ὅτι ἐρρήθη τοῖς ἀρχαίοις, and these sayings of 'men of old time' might fairly be summed up as παράδοσις or παραδοθέντα or perhaps νομιζόμενα.

We may now turn to the Saying proper, the answer to the four questions put by the disciples. None of the published restorations of the second half seems to be satisfactory. Dr Taylor seems to reconstruct the reply with little or no relevance to the questions of the disciples[5], and Prof. Swete's conjectures make only a remote answer, which fails to give any direction as to the manner of doing alms, of praying and of fasting: and the introduction of μυστήριον[6] seems specially arbi-

[1] This view is taken by GH, Swete and Taylor and is, I believe, generally accepted.
[2] *Ox. Pap.* IV p. 9.
[3] For this compound cp. *Gal.* iv 10 ἡμέρας παρατηρεῖσθε καὶ μῆνας καὶ καιρούς.
[4] Cp. *Mark* vii 4 (quoted above).
[5] Dr Taylor (*J. T. S.* VII p. 549) sees in l. 39 a reference to *Col.* iii 3 ἡ ζωὴ ὑμῶν κέκρυπται σὺν τῷ Χριστῷ ἐν τῷ Θεῷ.
[6] For which cp. *Col.* i 26 τὸ μ. τὸ ἀποκεκρυμμένον ἀπὸ τῶν αἰώνων.

trary. Here, as in the first half of the Saying, the Sermon on the Mount seems to be the best guide to restoration. The opening sections of *Matth.* vi on alms-giving, prayer and fasting are each accompanied by a warning, μὴ σαλπίσῃς...ὥσπερ οἱ ὑποκριταὶ ποιοῦσιν (*v.* 2); οὐκ ἔσεσθε ὡς οἱ ὑποκριταί (*v.* 5); μὴ γίνεσθε ὡς οἱ ὑποκριταί (*v.* 16), and in view of these some such restoration of the first half of l. 37 as Dr Taylor's appears inevitable.

The main answer to the dis-ciples' questions seems to lie in ll. 37–39, and if the questions themselves and the warning with which the reply opens appear to stand in intimate relation with the directions given in the Sermon on the Mount on Fasting, Prayer and Almsgiving, it is likely that the answer also should find a parallel in the same context. For the re-storation given in the text, I would compare: (1) *Matth.* vi 3–4 σοῦ δὲ ποιοῦντος ἐλεημοσύνην, μὴ γνώτω ἡ ἀριστερά σου τί ποιεῖ ἡ δεξιά σου· ὅπως ᾖ σου ἡ ἐλεημοσύνη ἐν τῷ κρυπτῷ (and the parallel passages, *vv.* 6 and 17), (2) *Matth.* vi 1 προσέχετε τὴν δικαιοσύνην ὑμῶν μὴ ποιεῖν ἔμπροσθεν τῶν ἀνθρώπων. In l. 38 ἀν[τέχεσθε was suggested to me, before I had seen Dr Taylor's reconstruction, by *Matth.* vi 24 and especially by *Isaiah* lvi 1 (quoted below): it being granted that ὑποκρ]ιταί (l. 37) is right, some such antithesis is required. The introduction of δικαιοσύνη which covers religious and moral observances is justified alike by *Matth.* vi 1 (just quoted) and by *Matth.* v 20, where the word is apparently equivalent to the ' Law and the Prophets.'

Lastly, the Saying clearly ends with the promise of a blessing on

those who comply with the direc-tion given above. The few letters extant in the papyrus are, of course, wholly inadequate of themselves to make any restoration probable ; but if, as we have seen reason to believe, the whole preceding part of the Saying is parallel to a defi-nite section of the Sermon on the Mount, our restoration, which re-lies upon the same passage, is at least plausible : cp. *Matth.* vi 1 προσέχετε...εἰ δὲ μήγε μισθὸν οὐκ ἔχετε παρὰ τῷ πατρὶ ὑμῶν τῷ ἐν τοῖς οὐρανοῖς: *ib.* 4 ὁ πατήρ σου ὁ βλέπων ἐν τῷ κρυπτῷ ἀποδώσει σοι ἐν τῷ φανερῷ[1]. The form of the blessing is perhaps dependent upon *Isaiah* lvi 2 μακάριος ἀνὴρ ὁ ποιῶν ταῦτα, καὶ ἄνθρωπος ὁ ἀντεχόμενος αὐτῶν[2]. For the introductory λέγω γάρ cp. *Matth.* v 20, 2 *Clem.* VIII 5.

The general correspondence of our Saying to the section of the Sermon on the Mount, accom-panied as it is by a marked freedom of treatment, raises the question of the relation between the logo-grapher and Matthew. The Ser-mon on the Mount is, as a whole, a highly edited document, and of no part of it is this more true than of the section which lies parallel to the Saying : the recurrence of the set form ' When ye...be not as the hypocrites who...: verily they have their reward. But when ye..., do it secretly. And the Father who seeth in secret shall reward you ' as each of the three great subjects is considered is an effective but essentially a literary device. The Saying, on the other hand, is quite informal and as we might think far more natural : ' How shall we do this and that ?' are answered not separately after one set form, but altogether. And it should be noted here that the disciples are

---

[1] ℵ, B, D, Z1 with some versions and witnesses omit the final phrase.
[2] Cp. also *Matth.* xxiv 46.

presumably bidden to keep τὰ παραδοθέντα : cp. *Matth.* xxiii 3, v 17–19.

Is it, then, possible that the Saying is an earlier and more original version of a part of the Sermon on the Mount ? A priori such a view is perhaps attractive, but it is hardly probable. The reply is cast in parallelistic form which is indeed a characteristic of many genuine Sayings, but in the Commentary on Saying IV we have already seen reason to suspect that parallelism may be the work of the author or editor upon whom the logographer drew ; and the presence of the word ἀλήθεια,

which is distinctly Johannine rather than Synoptic, forces us to believe that here again the parallelism is not a primary trait. And ingenious as is the shape into which the whole Saying is cast[1], such compression finds a parallel in [Athan.] λόγος σωτηρίας ix ad init. (p. 43, *ed.* von der Goltz) μηδεὶς καταμανθανέτω τὴν ἄσκησίν σου…ἀλλ᾿ εἴ τι ποιεῖς, ἐν κρυπτῷ ποίει. καὶ ὁ πατήρ σου ὁ οὐράνιος ὁ βλέπων ἐν τῷ κρυπτῷ ἀποδώσει σοι. Moreover, the correspondences of the Saying with Matthew and the differences from that parallel are just such as we find in other Sayings (*e.g.* Saying II) which are manifestly post-Synoptic.

SAYING VI

[Logion I]

a [λέγει Ἰ(ησοῦ)ς· ἔκβα-]
b [λε πρῶτον τὴν δοκὸν]
c [ἐκ τοῦ ὀφθαλμοῦ σου,]
  καὶ τότε διαβλέψεις
  ἐκβαλεῖν τὸ κάρφος
  τὸ ἐν τῷ ὀφθαλμῷ
  τοῦ ἀδελφοῦ σου.

a—c. LS (=*Luke* vi 42). ὀρύξεις | εἰς τὸ ἐνδότερόν σου τοῦ | ὀφθαλμοῦ τοῦ ἐκβα-|λεῖν τὴν ἐν αὐτῷ δοκόν |, *Bruston.* 1. διαβλέψειας, *Wessely*[2].

Jesus saith :

Cast out first the beam out of thine own eye,

And then thou shalt see clearly to cast out the mote that is in thy brother's eye.

[1] It was possibly suggested to him by *Luke* xi 1 ; and that incident might be thought a possible occasion for the present Saying.

[2] Wessely regards the ια (usually regarded as the page-number) as an alteration of διαβλέψεις.

The surviving fragment of this Saying stands first on the *verso* which the discoverers maintain to have come uppermost in the codex. The evidence on which their view is based[1] seems entirely satisfactory, and as it has already been reviewed in the Introduction, it need not be restated here. If Batiffol[2] were right in asserting the opposite view, the order of the Logia would be reversed, iv–viii becoming i–v : Bruston[3] actually accepts this inverted order and seeks to unite Logion I with Logion VIII, a change which carries with it a challenge of the discoverers' reading of the last two lines of the *recto*. This reconstruction cannot claim serious consideration unless examination of the papyrus should show Grenfell and Hunt's reading to be mistaken.

The Saying occurs in *Matth.* vii 3–5 and *Luke* vi 41–42 ; but there is nothing to show whether it appeared in our codex in the full form given by the Synoptics, or in the shorter form which LS[4] have suggested. The fragment as it stands agrees exactly with the *textus receptus* of *Luke* vi 42, and

that as Batiffol notes[5] in a minute point (τὸ ἐν τῷ ὀφθαλμῷ as against Matthew's ἐκ τοῦ ὀφθαλμοῦ). West-cott and Hort, however, following Codex Vaticanus (B) and some other MSS., put ἐκβαλεῖν at the end of the clause in preference to the other uncials and the Coptic version. Taylor has therefore sug-gested[6] that the extant portion may be derived from *Matth.* vii 3–5, the phrase τὸ κάρφος τὸ ἐν τῷ ὀφθαλμῷ being taken from *v.* 3, and the preceding part from *v.* 5. But such a hypothesis is as unlikely as it is artificial : surely it is both simple and natural to regard the fragment as identical with one of the two divergent lines of the Lucan text.

The Logion then must be derived from Luke or Luke's source (*i.e.* Q) ; but since on the one hand the Sayings and the Logia as a body are distinctly later than Luke, and on the other the phrase τὸ ἐν τῷ ὀφθαλμῷ is a literary refinement, such as we might well attribute to Luke himself, every consideration goes to show that the Saying derives from the Third Gospel.

SAYING VII
[LOGION II]

λέγει | Ἰ(ησοῦ)ς·

ἐὰν μὴ νηστεύση-   5

τε τὸν κόσμον, οὐ μὴ

εὕρητε τὴν βασιλεί-

αν τοῦ θ(εο)ῦ· καὶ ἐὰν μὴ

σαββατίσητε τὸ σάβ-

βατον, οὐκ ὄψεσθε τὸ(ν)   10

π(ατέ)ρα.

[1] Λόγια Ἰησοῦ pp. 6–7.
[3] *Les Paroles de Jésus* p. 10.
[5] *Op. cit.* p. 503.
[2] *Rev. Bibl.* 1897 pp. 501–2, 508–9.
[4] *Two Lectures* p. 7.
[6] *Oxyrhynchus Logia* pp. 6–7.

5–6. ΜΗ ΝΗϹΤΕΥϹΗΤΑΙ, *P.* μνηστεύσητε, *Kipp (ap.* Zahn), *Weiss*: μισήσητε, *von Gebhardt*: νηκήσητε (for νικήσητε), *Harnack*(?). τοῦ κόσμου, *LS*, *Gifford*: τῷ κόσμῳ, *Harnack*: εἰς τὸν κόσμον, *Redpath*: ἕως τῶν δυσμῶν, Anonym. in *Academy*: τοῦ κοινοῦ, *Quarry*: ἐλασμόν, *Davidson*: τὴν νηστείαν, *Cersoy*. 7. ΕΥΡΗΤΑΙ, *P.*

Jesus saith:

Except ye fast toward the world, ye shall not find the King-dom of God;

And unless ye sanctify the whole week, ye shall not see the Father.

The reading of the papyrus is sufficiently clear throughout, but the unusual νηστεύσητε τὸν κόσμον has very generally been treated as a blunder. Yet none of the emendations proposed is satisfactory. The association of κόσμος with νηστεύειν or its equivalent ἀποτάξεσθαι is well enough attested to put out of court all attempts to change either verb or noun: thus Clement of Alexandria[1] has μα-κάριοι...οἱ τοῦ κόσμου νηστεύοντες, and οὕτως καὶ ἡμεῖς τῶν κοσμικῶν νηστεύειν χρή: and in *Acta Pauli et Theclae*[2] we have μακάριοι οἱ ἀποταξάμενοι τῷ κόσμῳ τούτῳ, and again in *Pistis Sophia*[3] 'ἀποτάσ-σετε κόσμῳ omni et ὕλῃ omni.' Others have tried to alter the accusative, Harnack suggesting the dative, Lock and Gifford the genitive. This last would at least bring the phrase into line with Clement's use; but the laws of parallelism certainly require an ac-cusative after νηστεύειν to balance σάββατον. Cersoy[4] has sought another solution of the difficulty and one which is very attractive: the Aramaic words answering to κόσμος and νηστεία are so closely similar that a confusion of the two

would be the easiest matter pos-sible. If, therefore, the Sayings, or the document from which they were derived, have been translated from the Aramaic, a translator working in the earlier part of the second century would the more easily fall into this error from his knowledge of the current expres-sion 'to fast from the world.' The correction of κόσμον to νηστείαν would have the advantage of per-fecting the parallelism, νηστεύειν τὴν νηστείαν exactly balancing σαββατίζειν τὸ σάββατον. How-ever attractive this view may be, other considerations seem to make it inadmissible; for the supposed translator would surely have written τοῦ κόσμου had he been thinking of the current ν. τοῦ κόσμου. And the proposed change radically alters the meaning of the Saying, attri-buting to Jesus a rigid formalism of which we have no other evidence and which is improbable in itself[5]. Even granted that the Logion is taken from the *Gospel according to the Hebrews*[6], it would be difficult to believe that the compiler of that book could have so far misrepre-sented the teaching of Jesus. If we are to accept Cersoy's sugges-

[1] *Strom.* III 15. 99.   [2] § v.   [3] P. 157 [250] ed. Petermann.
[4] *Rev. Bibl.* 1898 pp. 415–16.
[5] But cp. *Matth.* 'one jot or one tittle shall in no wise pass from the law until all be fulfilled.'
[6] Since this Gospel satisfied Christian adherents to the old Law (Euseb. *H.E.* III 27 4).

tion at all, we must suppose that the Saying either belongs to an early period in the ministry before the characteristic antagonism to formalism had been developed —which is improbable in view of the references to the Father and to the Kingdom of God, signs which indicate a more mature period—, or was intended to correct a tendency to carry customary religious observances too lightly. In favour of this last compare *Matth.* v 18, 19.

The construction νηστεύειν τὸν κόσμον is certainly unusual, but seems defensible[1]. Matthew (v 6) has οἱ πεινῶντες καὶ διψῶντες τὴν δικαιοσύνην where the accusative is not the object of the participles, but expresses that in respect of which men hunger or thirst[2]; similarly νηστεύειν τὸν κόσμον surely means 'to be fasting in regard to (towards) the world[3].' Further, Professor Bevan[4] has cited the Arabic: 'If thou desirest to escape the chastisement of God, then fast the world' (صَمِ الدُّنْيَا). The shade of thought conveyed by the phrase in question deserves closer examination. When Clement of Alexandria uses νηστεύειν τοῦ κόσμου, his meaning is clearly 'to abstain from all that characterises the world as opposed to the heavenly kingdom': he uses νηστεύειν metaphorically. In the Logion, however, νηστεύειν retains its literal sense in part: fasting is merely symbolical and so, in itself, worth nothing; it must be in respect of the world, of evil things.

The emphasis, so to say, is on κόσμον, which introduces a new element, while the verb carries the old idea of fasting (abstinence from food) which is to be developed in the new direction.

The second half of the parallelism has caused some difficulty, though less than the first. Most editors are forced to use σαββατίζειν τὸ σάββατον in a sense which has no parallel, 'to keep *true* sabbath,' or the like. Taylor[5] after collecting the LXX uses of σαββατίζειν concludes that 'in no case does "to sabbathize a sabbath" mean to keep the Sabbath in the ordinary sense,' and that the Logion inculcates something altogether different from keeping the Jewish Sabbath in the ordinary way. Now, followed by σάββατον, σάββατα, the verb means either 'to keep the sabbatical year,' or 'to keep the Day of Atonement' (*Levit.* xxiii 32). The first of these senses is obviously out of the question here: the second would force us to accept Cersoy's correction in the first part of the Saying, since on the Day of Atonement the ideas of Fast and Sabbath were specially connected[6]. That the Saying[7] merely laid stress on keeping the Day of Atonement is, however, to narrow it beyond the limits we can admit, and if σαββατίζειν τὸ σ. means only 'to keep the Day of Atonement,' it no longer balances νηστεύειν τοῦ κόσμου.

Early Christian writers develop the idea of a spiritual Sabbath as opposed to the formal Jewish institution, and of these the most

---

[1] Taylor (*J.T.S.* VII p. 549) points out that a similar accusative is used in I *Cor.* vii 31 οἱ χρώμενοι τὸν κόσμον ὡς μὴ καταχρώμενοι.
[2] The A.V. rendering 'they who hunger and thirst *after* righteousness' is therefore incorrect: '*toward* righteousness' might be better.
[3] Wessely renders 'fast in that which concerns the world,' and regards the phrase as equivalent to ἀποτάσσεσθαι τῷ κόσμῳ: cp. *Luke* xiv 33. See also Empedocles *ap.* Plutarch *De Cohibenda Ira* (*ad fin.*) νηστεύειν κακότητος.
[4] Darembourg-Spiro, *Chrestomathie* (ed. 2) p. 34: see Taylor *J.T.S.* III 549.
[5] *Ox. Log.* pp. 13–14.   [6] *Ib.* pp. 15 sqq.
[7] It may have been uttered on the Day of Atonement.

SAYINGS OF JESUS　29

important in the present connection is Justin, who writes[1] : σαββατίζειν ὑμᾶς ὁ καινὸς νόμος διὰ
παντὸς ἐθέλει, καὶ ὑμεῖς μίαν ἀργοῦντες ἡμέραν εὐσεβεῖν δοκεῖτε, μὴ
νοοῦντες διὰ τί ὑμῖν προσετάγη.
He then goes on to show that the
true Sabbath consists in ceasing to
sin and concludes: καὶ σεσαβ-
βάτικε τὰ τρυφερὰ καὶ ἀληθινὰ
σάββατα τοῦ θεοῦ. Here the words
μίαν ἀργοῦντες ἡμέραν are particularly important, implying, as they
do, censure of the Jewish practice
of observing one day formally to
the neglect of other days, whereas
the new law bids men hold Sabbath διὰ παντός. Now, as in the
first half of the Saying, so here the
verb retains in a large measure
its customary sense, and the object
indicates the direction in which the
old ordinance is to be developed.
σάββατον, consequently, is not
used in its ordinary sense here,
but means 'week,' a use which is
well attested : cp. Luke xviii 12
νηστεύω δὶς τοῦ σαββάτου ; John
xx 1, 19 ; 1 Cor. xvi 2 κατὰ μίαν
σαββάτου ; Didache viii 1 νηστεύ-
ουσι γὰρ δευτέρᾳ σαββάτων καὶ
πέμπτῃ. The word σάββατον was
used in this sense commonly enough
to have passed into Coptic; for in a
collection of Sayings of the Fathers [2]
we read 'they of Shiêt fasted
the whole week' (ⲡⲥⲁⲃⲃⲁⲧⲟⲛ
ⲧⲏⲣϥ) while the corresponding
Greek version[3] has αὐτοὶ δὲ οἱ Σκη-
τιῶται ἐνήστευον τὴν ἑβδομάδα.
The general idea of this part of
the Saying, therefore, will be : the
observance of one day in the week
as holy is symbolical ; and if this
fact is forgotten, Sabbath-keeping
degenerates into fetichism — the
cult of one day on which certain
standards are in force which do
not apply to other days. The new
law requires men to sanctify, or

make a Sabbath of, each day of
the week.
The Saying as a whole is independent, but is not without
Synoptic relations. It may be conjectured that it was uttered on
some such occasion as that to
which the group of incidents recorded in Luke v 33–vi 11 belong :
there the question of fasting is
discussed, to be followed by two
episodes directed against formalism
in Sabbath-keeping. Yet it is important to observe that there is a
distinct post-Synoptic shade in the
teaching of the Logion, which
urges a reapplication of the existing religious observances, while
the protest of the Synoptic Jesus
is against the exclusion of good or
necessary work on the Sabbath,
and against ostentation in fasting.
The general sense of the Logion,
as also its form, is best paralleled
by Matth. v 20 ἐὰν μὴ περισ-
σεύσῃ ἡ δικαιοσύνη ὑμῶν πλεῖον τῶν
γραμματέων καὶ Φαρισαίων, οὐ μὴ
εἰσέλθητε εἰς τὴν βασιλείαν τῶν
οὐρανῶν, where not only is the last
clause strikingly close to the apodoses of the Logion, but the
'righteousness of the Scribes and
Pharisees' is to be taken to mean
just such things as fasting and
Sabbath-keeping. One is tempted
to conjecture that the Saying was
developed in the atmosphere of
later thought from this passage with
the aid of particulars borrowed
from the Lucan passage noticed
just above. At least such a method
would be just what we might
expect (cp. Saying IV, Logia VI
and VII). The apparent Synoptic element in the protases—to
which must be added the formula
ἐὰν μή introducing conditions of
salvation—is still more obvious
in the apodoses. Harnack[4] has
shown this most fully : ἡ βασιλεία

[1] Dialog. c. Tryph. 12.　　　[2] Rev. de l'Orient Chrét. XVIII p. 178 (no. 171).
[3] Id. XIV p. 363 (no. 242).
[4] Die jüngst entdeckten Sprüche Jesu p. 8.

τοῦ θεοῦ is of course Synoptic (*Matth.* xix 24); εὑρίσκειν is not actually used in connection with βασιλεία by the Synoptics, but we have the corresponding ζητεῖτε τὴν βασιλείαν (*Matth.* vi 33, *Luke* xii 31) and ζητεῖτε καὶ εὑρήσετε (*Matth.* vii 7). In the second apodosis, however, οὐκ ὄψεσθε τὸν πατέρα has a distinctly Johannine ring (*John* xiv 9 ἑώρακε τὸν πατέρα), though both the verb and the absolute use of ὁ πατήρ have Synoptic parallels (*Matth.* v 8 αὐτοὶ τὸν θεὸν ὄψονται, *id.* xi 27 οὐδεὶς ἐπιγινώσκει τὸν υἱὸν εἰ μὴ ὁ 'πατήρ). The use of κόσμος deepens this impression of Johannine influence : cp. 1 *John* ii 15 μὴ ἀγαπᾶτε τὸν κόσμον μηδὲ τὰ ἐν τῷ κόσμῳ. The Logion therefore has a peculiar technical, as apart from an intrinsic, value. It is indebted chiefly to the Synoptics : Johannine influence is apparent, but certainly not dominant ; and we would conclude that the Logographer while post-Synoptic, wrote at a period when Johannine thought was only nascent, or, perhaps, in a locality to which only echoes of that movement had reached. The peculiar shade of thought which we have traced is probably characteristic of the period in which the Saying received its definite form : in its attitude towards fasting and Sabbath-keeping it lies somewhere between the Synoptics and Clement of Alexandria, nearer perhaps to the latter than the former.

Clement of Alexandria[1] develops from *Isaiah* lviii 6–14 the idea of a spiritual Sabbath in contradistinction to the Jewish institution[2] in a passage which has been thought to imply a knowledge of this Saying or of something intimately related to it. εὐνοῦχος τοίνυν...ὁ ἄγονος ἀληθείας. ξύλον οὗτος ξηρὸν ἦν πρότερον· ὑπακούσας δὲ τῷ λόγῳ, καὶ

φυλάξας τὰ σάββατα κατ᾽ ἀποχὴν ἁμαρτημάτων ... ἐντιμότερος ἔσται τῶν ἄνευ πολιτείας ὀρθῆς λόγῳ μόνῳ παιδευομένων. διὰ τοῦτο 'οὐκ εἰσελεύσεται εὐνοῦχος εἰς ἐκκλησίαν θεοῦ,' ὁ ἄγονος καὶ ἄκαρπος καὶ πολιτείᾳ καὶ λόγῳ, ἀλλ᾽ οἱ μὲν εὐνουχίσαντες ἑαυτοὺς ἀπὸ πάσης ἁμαρτίας διὰ τὴν βασιλείαν τῶν οὐρανῶν· μακάριοι οὗτοί εἰσιν οἱ τοῦ κόσμου νηστεύοντες. Robinson[3] holds that Clement is here making use of the second Logion (φυλάξας τὰ σάββατα...μακάριοι οὗτοί εἰσιν οἱ τοῦ κόσμου νηστεύοντες) which he found in the *Gospel according to the Egyptians*, and that later on he adapts the fifth Logion from the same source. Both in the Introduction (pp. xl ff.) and in the Commentary on Logion v I have given reason for rejecting the attribution of the Logia to the Egyptian Gospel : in this place it will be sufficient to point out that, while there is nothing to show any connection between Clement's references to 'keeping Sabbath' and to 'they who fast from the world,' his source was certainly not our Logion in that the beatitude μακάριοι...εἰσιν οἱ τοῦ κόσμου νηστεύοντες is certainly a direct quotation[4], as is clear from *Strom.* III i 4 εἰ γὰρ ἦν παρὰ θεοῦ..ἡ τοιαύτη διασκευή, οὐκ ἂν ἐμακάρισέν τοὺς εὐνούχους. And that apocryphal literature produced such beatitudes, it will be sufficient to quote *Acta Pauli et Theclae* § 5 μακάριοι οἱ ἀποταξάμενοι τῷ κόσμῳ τούτῳ. We conclude, then, that while Dr Robinson may well be right in urging that in the passage quoted above, Clement has his eye fixed upon the Egyptian Gospel, our Logion was different from his source both in form and—if our interpretation of the Logion is on the right lines—in the shade of its meaning.

---

[1] *Strom.* III 15 § 99, quoted by Professor Mayor *ap.* Rendel Harris *Contemporary Review* 1897.
[2] *Cp.* LS p. 9.   [3] *Expositor* 1897 pp. 417 sqq.   [4] In imitation of *Isaiah* lvi 1.

SAYING VIII

[LOGION III]

λέγει 'Ι(ησοῦ)ς· ἔ[σ]την
ἐν μέσῳ τοῦ κόσμου,
καὶ ἐν σαρκὶ ὤφθην
αὐτοῖς· καὶ εὖρον πάν-
τας μεθύοντας, καὶ   15
οὐδένα εὖρον δειψῶ(ν)-
τα ἐν αὐτοῖς· καὶ πο-
νεῖ ἡ ψυχή μου ἐπὶ
τοῖς υἱοῖς τῶν ἀν(θρώπ)ων,
ὅτι τυφλοί εἰσιν τῇ καρ-   20
δίᾳ αὐτῶ(ν), κạị̣ [οὐ] βλέπ-
[ουσι τῇ διανοίᾳ αὐτῶν].

13. ϹΑΡΚΕΙ, *P* (corrected by the original hand) : ἔτι ἐν σαρκὶ ᾖ,
Bruston. 21. Κạị̣...ΒΛΕΙϹ, *GH* : καὶ οὐ βλέπουσιν οὐδὲ γινώσκουσιν τὴν
ἑαυτῶν πτωχίαν, *Swete* (combining with Logion IV) : καὶ οὐ βλέπουσιν,
πτωχοὶ καὶ οὐκ οἴδασιν τὴν πτωχίαν, *Cross* : κ. ο. β. τὴν ταλαιπωρίαν
αὐτῶν καὶ τὴν πτωχίαν, *Taylor* : ἀμβλεῖς τῷ νοΐ, *Zahn* : ἀ. τῷ νῷ αὐτῶν,
Davidson : ἀ. τῇ διανοίᾳ καὶ οὐκ οἴδασιν αὐτῶν τὴν πτωχίαν, *Lock* :
ἀμβλεῖς, μὴ γεινώσκοντες ἑαυτῶν τὴν πτωχίαν, *Sanday* : καὶ βραδεῖς τῇ
ἀκοῇ αὐτῶν· ἀλλὰ διώκετε τὴν πτωχίαν, *Heinrici* : καὶ οὐ βλέποντες,
Bruston.

Jesus saith :
I stood in the midst of the world, And in flesh was I seen of
  them ;
And I found all men drunken, And none found I athirst among
  them ;
And my soul grieveth over the sons of men,
Because they are blind in their heart, And see not with their
  understanding.

The length of the lacuna after
l. 21 has been a matter of dispute.
Most editors and critics have not
found strength to resist the temptation to join the remains of Logion IV
to Logion III, and so argue that
little more than a line or two has
been lost at the foot of the *verso*[1].
Of the restorations based on this
assumption, that of Mr Cross[2] is
by far the best, as brilliantly con-
tinuing the parallelistic form.
Taylor's reconstruction while rest-
ing on *Apoc.* iii 17 shows less clear-
cut parallelism. On the other side,
the discoverers claim that as many
as five lines or even more may
have been lost[3]; and in a codex of
this date the page is likely to have
resembled the column of the roll
in its proportions. I have therefore
not attempted to unite Logia III
and IV, and, since l. 21 almost
certainly concludes with καὶ [οὐ]
βλέπ᾽[ουσι][4], have ended the Saying
with τῇ διανοίᾳ αὐτῶν[5] which
balances the τῇ καρδίᾳ αὐτῶν of
ll. 20–1. For the parallelism τυφλοί
εἰσι...οὐ βλέπουσι cp. *Acts* xiii 11
τυφλὸς ἔσει...μὴ βλέπων τὸν ἥλιον.
   The two opening clauses of the
Logion are closely parallel to
Baruch iii 28 μετὰ τοῦτο ἐπὶ τῆς
γῆς ὤφθη, καὶ ἐν τοῖς ἀνθρώποις
συνανεστράφη, and literary dependence seems quite certain, in view
of the fact remarked by GH[6] that
some of the Fathers[7] applied this
passage to the life of Jesus. The
discoverers are inclined further to
see a connection between the words
ἐν μέσῳ τοῦ κόσμου and the *agraphon*[8] 'hic est medium mundi,'
but the phrase in the Logion

certainly has no local or mystic
meaning, and, as the parallelism
shows, means no more than αὐτοῖς,
'among men.'
   The aorists ἔστην, ὤφθην, εὗρον
are thought by Harnack[9] to indicate a form of Logos doctrine
implying pre-existence as in *John*
xvi 28 ἐξῆλθον ἐκ τοῦ πατρὸς καὶ
ἐλήλυθα εἰς τὸν κόσμον. Batiffol[10]
on the contrary sees in them the
doctrine of post-existence, and
thinks that there is here Docetism
such as that of the *Acta Johannis*.
But surely the aorists indicate past
actions and not past states, while
the present, πονεῖ (which leads
Batiffol to split the Logion in two),
indicates the speaker's consequent
state of feeling at the moment of
utterance. The meaning, then,
will be: 'I took my place among
men (*sc.* at the *beginning* of my
ministry), and now, after ex-
periencing the ways of men, my
soul grieves.' Moreover, πονεῖ ἡ
ψυχή μου would be most inappropriate in a post-resurrectional
Saying; and ἐν σαρκί while it
implies pre-existence does not
emphasise that doctrine, but dwells
rather on the humanity of Jesus[11],
as a reason why men ought to have
been able to understand and accept
him: we might paraphrase 'as a
man among men' (cp. the Saying
quoted by Origen διὰ τοὺς ἀσθενοῦν-
τας ἠσθένουν, καὶ διὰ τοὺς πεινῶντας
ἐπείνων, καὶ διὰ τοὺς διψῶντας ἐδί-
ψων[12]).
   The words μεθύοντας...διψῶντα
are regarded by Canon Sanday as
marks of Encratite influence: διψᾶν,
he argues, is used only once by

[1] LS p. 38.
[2] *Expositor* 1897 p. 259.
[3] *Ox. Pap.* I p. 1.
[4] *Ib.* p. 3.
[5] For this expression cp. 2 *Clem.* I 6 πηροὶ ὄντες τῇ διανοίᾳ.
[6] Λόγια Ἰησοῦ p. 12.
[7] *E.g.* Irenaeus *Adv. Haeres.* IV xxxiv 4 (ed. Harvey).
[8] Resch *Agrapha* pp. 457 ff.   [9] *Die jüngst entdeckten Sprüche Jesu* p. 14.
[10] *Rev. Bibl.* 1897 pp. 507–8. Taylor (*J.T.S.* VII 550) seems to take the same
view, that Jesus is represented as looking back after the Resurrection to the days of
his flesh: he compares *Hebr.* v 7 ἐν ταῖς ἡμέραις τῆς σαρκὸς αὐτοῦ.
[11] As, perhaps, in *Barn.* v εἰ γὰρ μὴ ἦλθεν ἐν σαρκί, πῶς ἂν ἐσώθημεν ἄνθρωποι;
[12] Preuschen *Antilegomena* p. 28 12.

a Synoptic writer (*Matth.* v 6) in a spiritual sense, while in the fourth Gospel " the sense is always made clear by the context "; for the technical use of μεθύειν he can find no parallel. This view seems rather extreme. Any reader, especially one who had the slightest acquaintance with Johannine phraseology, could not fail to grasp the meaning of διψῶντα, which is as clear here as in *John* vii 37 ἐάν τις διψᾷ ἐρχέσθω πρός με καὶ πινέτω[1]. But here again I think we have a literary debt to *Isaiah* lv 1 οἱ διψῶντες πορεύεσθε ἐφ' ὕδωρ. If so, we may perhaps discern not developed but incipient Johannism at work, just as in the earlier clauses the Logos doctrine is rudimentary as compared with its presentment in the fourth Gospel. Similarly μεθύοντας need not be Encratite, but is again perfectly clear in the light of *Isaiah* xxviii 1 οὐαὶ τῷ στεφάνῳ τῆς ὕβρεως, οἱ μισθωτοὶ Ἐφραίμ...οἱ μεθύοντες ἄνευ οἴνου. In the Logion, however, men are not represented as drunken with ὕβρις; and *Luke* xxi 34 προσέχετε δὲ ἑαυτοῖς μήποτε βαρηθῶσιν ὑμῶν αἱ καρδίαι ἐν κραιπάλῃ καὶ μέθῃ καὶ μερίμναις βιωτικαῖς, may have been in the compiler's mind[2]. Compare further *Matth.* xxiv 38 f. (= *Luke* xvii 26) ὥσπερ γὰρ ἦσαν ἐν ταῖς ἡμέραις ἐκείναις (*sc.* of Noah) τρώγοντες καὶ πίνοντες, γαμοῦντες καὶ ἐκγαμίζοντες...οὕτως ἔσται ἡ παρουσία τοῦ υἱοῦ τοῦ ἀνθρώπου, and v 50 (cp. *Luke* xii 45) where eating and drinking μετὰ τῶν μεθυόντων are amongst the sins of the Wicked Servant. Probably, therefore, both Old Testament and Synoptic influences are blended in this part of the Saying.

Batiffol, as we have seen, pro-

poses to meet the change of tense from aorist (ἔστην) to present (πονεῖ) by dividing the Logion into two Sayings of which the second begins with πονεῖ ἡ ψυχή, καί being editorial. He supports this view by the following considerations: (1) the change of tense indicates two different occasions; (2) the first four clauses form a complete parallelism which would be disturbed were the πονεῖ clause truly a part of the same Saying; (3) the lack of antithesis between this and the preceding clauses. It has been shown already that the change of tense is accounted for by the sense, and surely it is perfectly natural to find the πονεῖ clause following the four earlier clauses; for the first part of the Saying, a complaint against the attitude of men, would seem incomplete without a following statement of the result upon the feelings of Jesus. Thirdly, the πονεῖ clause does indeed stand outside the parallelism, but the same thing occurs in *Matth.* vii 3–4, where the clause 'or how shalt thou say to thy brother' occupies an exactly similar position[3]: and the isolation of this clause gives it the special prominence which it deserves. Dr Abbott has aptly quoted the Sibylline Oracle[4]:
καὶ τότε δ' Ἰσραὴλ μεμεθυσμένος
οὐχὶ νοήσει,
...ἀτὰρ ὄμμασιν οὐκ ἐσορῶντες
τυφλότεροι σπαλάκων,
which possibly stands in some relation to this Logion and, if so, fortifies its unity by the association of the ideas of drunkenness and blindness. Similarly Reitzenstein[5] quotes pseudo-Hermes Trismegistus: ποῖ φέρεσθε ὦ ἄνθρωποι, μεθύοντες, τὸν τῆς ἀγνωσίας ἄκρατον (λόγον) ἐκπιόντες...; στῆτε νήψαντες,

---

[1] Cp. also *Apoc.* xxi 6 ἐγὼ τῷ διψῶντι δώσω ἐκ τῆς πηγῆς τοῦ ὕδατος τῆς ζωῆς δωρεάν, which again surely recalls *Isaiah* lv 1.
[2] Cf. also *Luke* viii 14.
[3] Cf. also λέγω γάρ in Saying v, if our restoration is right.   [4] 1 360, 370.
[5] *Poimandres* p. 204.

W.   3

ἀναβλέψατε τοῖς ὀφθαλμοῖς τῆς καρδίας. But it seems unnecessary to see here the influence of Egyptian syncretism.

The general character of the second part of the Logion is quite Synoptic: compare *Matth.* xxiii 37; *Luke* xiii 34, xix 41 (cited by Harnack). *John* i 10–11 and the *Apocrypha* 'qui mecum sunt non me intellexerunt,' πολλάκις ἐπεθύμησα ἀκοῦσαι ἕνα τῶν λόγων τούτων καὶ οὐκ ἔσχον τὸν ἐροῦντα[1], are animated by the same feeling. The phrase πονεῖ ἡ ψυχή μου is certainly to be attributed to *Isaiah* liii 10 καὶ βούλεται κύριος ἀφελεῖν ἀπὸ τοῦ πονοῦ τῆς ψυχῆς αὐτοῦ, and Harnack also quotes *Matth.* xxvi 38, *Mark* xiv 34, *John* xii 27 for trouble of soul in Jesus. The occasion of the Saying must have been similar to that of *Matth.* xiii 58, *Mark* vi 6 or *Matth.* xv.

In the two final clauses of the Logion the idea of spiritual sight or blindness finds an exact parallel in the *Gospel according to Thomas*[2], νῦν καρποφορείτωσαν τὰ σά, καὶ βλεπέτωσαν οἱ τυφλοὶ τῇ καρδίᾳ; but its virtual equivalent is common, as in *Psalms* lxviii (lxix) 24,

Matth. xv 14, xxiii 16, *John* ix 39 (quoted by Harnack)[3]. Compare also *Luke* iv 18 κηρῦξαι... τυφλοῖς ἀνάβλεψιν (cited from *Isaiah*).

As a result of this examination we can trace three lines of influence in the Saying. Hebrew literature has left a deep mark, and to this must be added the Hebraisms πονεῖ ἐπὶ and υἱοὶ ἀνθρώπων[4], the repeated use of καί to introduce each clause, and the parallelistic form. The opening clauses of the Logion betray a tendency to Messianic interpretation later than that of the Synoptics. Secondly, the latter part of the Saying is Synoptic alike in the character of its thought, and in the simple directness and depth of its expression. Johannine characteristics, lastly, are perhaps not so prominent as they have been thought to be; yet the use of μεθύειν and διψᾶν, while not un-Synoptic and probably derived from the Old Testament itself, suggests that the Logion was formulated in an atmosphere not wholly free from Johannine metaphorical phraseology.

SAYING IX
[LOGION IV]

[λέγει 'Ι(ησοῦ)ς· ...]
*   *   *   *

[....]ει[ν τ]ὴν πτωχεία(ν).

22. πτωχ[ία, *P*.   22–3. καλὸν ἀν(θρώπ)ῳ τὴν πτ. | αἱρεῖσθαι οὗ ἐὰν κ.τ.λ., *and* κελεύω σοι ἵνα τὴν πτ. προήρησαι ὅπου ἐὰν κ.τ.λ., *Bruston.*

Jesus saith:
*   *   * to...(their?) poverty.

[1] Preuschen *Antileg.* pp. 30–2.   [2] A VIII (ed. Tischendorf).
[3] For its use in early Christian literature cf. 1 *Clement* xxxvi ἠνεώχθησαν ἡμῶν οἱ ὀφθαλμοὶ τῆς καρδίας, and 2 *Clem.* I 6 (quoted above).
[4] Harnack *op. cit.* p. 13.

The restorations which connect this fragment with the preceding Saying have been discussed already in the Commentary on Logion III. Bruston's attempts to unite this with the succeeding Logion rest on certain corrections[1] of the discoverers' readings made, apparently, without a re-examination of the original, and for that reason alone cannot be considered seriously. The obvious fact that ll. 23–30 form a single Saying for which we have parallels, and in which the idea of poverty has no place, puts his reconstructions completely out of court.

GH observe that πτωχεία does not occur in any recorded Saying of Jesus, and that the Logion is, therefore, probably new. Yet this occasion may have been Synoptic, for πτωχοί occurs frequently, and we might perhaps think of the incident of the woman with the alabastron of myrrh (*Matth.* xxvi 11) as a possible occasion for the fragment: the Saying may have concluded: 'Ye have the poor with you always, and when ye will ye are able to relieve their poverty' [κουφίζ]ει[ν τ]ὴν πτω-χείαν.

SAYING X

[LOGION V]

[λέγ]ει ['Ι(ησοῦ)ς·
        ὅπ]ου ἐὰν ὦσιν
[β', οὐκ] ε[ἰσι]ν ἄθεοι· καὶ
[ὅ]που ε[ἷς] ἐστιν μόνος,   25
[λέ]γω ἐγώ εἰμι μετ' αὐ-
τ[οῦ]. ἔγει[ρ]ον τὸν λίθο(ν),
κἀκεῖ εὑρήσεις με,
σχίσον τὸ ξύλον, κἀγὼ
ἐκεῖ εἰμι.   30

23–26. [...]ει [....]ου εαν ωcιν [....] ε[...]ν. θεοι και [..]ϛο· ε[..] εcτιν μονοc [..]τω εϝω ειμι κ.τ.λ., *P*: λέγει Ἰ(ησοῦ)ς· ὅπου ἐὰν ὦσιν....ε.....θεοι καὶ ..ϛο· ε.. ἐστιν μόνος ..τω ἐγώ ειμι, *GH*: ὅπου ἐὰν ὦσιν β̄, οὐκ εἰσιν ἄθεοι, καὶ ὅπου εἷς ἐστιν μόνος, λέγω ἐγώ εἰμι, *Blass*: ὅπου ἐὰν ὦσιν οὐκ εἰσιν ἄθεοι καὶ ὥσπερ εἷς, *Harnack*: ὅ. ἐ. ὦ. ἄνδρες καὶ ἄθεοι καὶ εἴ που εἷς, *Cross*: ὅ. ἐ. ὦ. πάντες μισόθεοι καὶ πιστὸς εἷς, *Swete*: ὅ. ἐ. ὦ. δύο, ἐκεῖ...οι καὶ ἐγώ. οὗ εἷς, *Heinrici*: ὅ. ἐ. ὦ. οἱ λεγόμενοι θεοί, *Redpath*: ὅ. ἐ. ὦ. ἔνιοι ἄθεοι καὶ ὅσιος εἷς, *von Gebhardt*: ὅ. ἐ. ὦ. λίαν ἰσχυροὶ οἱ ἄθεοι καὶ ἐν τῇ δόξῃ τις ἐστιν μόνος ἑαυτῷ, and ὅ. ἐ. ὦ. αὐτῷ ἐχθροὶ ἄθεοι καὶ ἄν(θρωπ)ος ὃς ἐκεῖ ἐστιν μόνος οὕτω, *Bruston*

[1] *Paroles de Jésus* pp. 7, 15–16, 21.

36   *SAYINGS OF JESUS*

(with Saying IX prefixed in both cases): ὅ. ἑ. ὤ. β΄ ἤ γ΄, ἐκεῖ εἰσιν μετὰ
θεοῦ, καὶ εἴ που εἷς ἐστιν μόνος, ἰδοὺ ἐγώ εἰμι μετ᾽ αὐτοῦ, *Jülicher.*
26. [..]τω, *P*: λέγω, *Blass*[1], *Redpath, Cross*: αὐτῷ, *Clemen*: αὐτῷ,
Zahn, Reitzenstein, Blass[2]: ἰδού, *Swete*: ἐκεῖ, *Heinrici*: οὕτω, *Harnack*:
αὐτοῦ, *von Gebhardt*: ζήτω, *Badham*: κάτω, *Davidson.*   27. ἐξᾶρον,
Harnack, Bruston: ἔγξισον (*for* ἔγξυσον) *Wessely.*

Jesus saith :
Wheresoever there be two, they are not without God,
And where there is one alone, I say, I am with him.
Lift up the stone, and there thou shalt find me ;
Cleave the wood, and there I am.

For the actual reading of the papyrus reference must be made to the exhaustive note of the discoverers[1]. Blass' brilliant restoration is certainly final: its central point is, of course, the conjecture β΄ (δύο), and that 'Two' is here required is certain in view of the extant parallels to the first part of the Saying to be noticed presently. Objection has been raised[2] to the use of a cipher in a literary text and side by side with a number which is written out in full; but there are parallels which sufficiently cover this use. A papyrus fragment of St Matthew[3] has πᾶσαι οὖν γε[νε]αὶ ἀπὸ Ἀβραὰμ ἕως Δαυὶδ γενεαὶ ιδ̄. Mr Redpath has drawn attention to the fact that in a MS. like Codex B of the LXX ciphers are frequently found alongside the full word, as in *Num.* xxviii 19 μόσχους δύο, κριὸν ἕνα, ἀμνοὺς ἐνιαυσίους ζ΄, and Dr Sanday[4] points to the variants in *Acts* xxvii 37 as evidence for the use of ciphers in a literary text. But a far more satisfactory parallel is forthcoming in the recently published fragment

of *Tobit*[5] where we find (ll. 2 ff.) ἐγώ εἰμι Ῥαφαὴλ εἷς ἐκ τῶν ζ΄ ἀγίων, and again (ll. 7 f.) ἐταράχθησαν οἱ β΄ καὶ ἔπεσον ἐπὶ πρόσωπον. Since, therefore, Blass' restoration is so strongly supported and in itself is so entirely satisfactory, it is unnecessary to discuss the other and less adequate conjectures which have been put forward.

The Saying is in two parts, the second of which is wholly new, while the first seems to stand in some relation to the canonical scriptures, and has parallels more or less close in citations from non-canonical documents.

The most obvious parallel to the first part is *Matth.* xviii 20 οὗ γάρ εἰσι δύο ἢ τρεῖς συνηγμένοι εἰς τὸ ἐμὸν ὄνομα, ἐκεῖ εἰμι ἐν μέσῳ αὐτῶν, and there can be no doubt that the relation is real[6]. Yet it is characteristic of the Logion that it sounds a distinct note: while Matthew by the addition of συνηγμένοι κ.τ.λ. makes the promised presence conditional on a formal gathering or congregation, the Saying has a diametrically opposite

[1] Λόγια Ἰησοῦ p. 13.
[2] *Ox. Pap.* I p. 2.
[3] *Ox. Pap.* I no. 2 (recto, l. 9).
[4] *Two Lectures*, p. 39.
[5] *Oxyrhynchus Papyri* no. 1594 (pt XIII).
[6] Taylor (*J. T. S.* VII p. 550) regards the first clause as dependent upon the Matthaean tradition, and the second clause concerning the 'one alone' as an 'appendix to an appendix'; Wessely considers that the development of the Matthaean original was due to Egyptian pantheistic influence: cp. Reitzenstein *Poimandres* p. 240.

tendency[1], and affirms that Jesus will be with his followers however lonely they may be, or in however informal circumstances. The spirit of the Logion-version, though not its form, is more nearly approached by *Matth.* xxviii 20 καὶ ἰδού, ἐγὼ μεθ' ὑμῶν εἰμι πάσας τὰς ἡμέρας ἕως τῆς συντελείας τῆς αἰῶνος: and, though it contains no reference to solitude, the absence of the frigid ceremonial condition suffices to place this Saying on the same level as the Oxyrhynchus 'Logion.' Since the Saying cannot be assumed to be more true historically than the Matthaean parallel first quoted, it is probable that it is a conscious correction or amplification of that utterance, inspired, possibly, by the wider spirit of the second Matthaean parallel and (I would add) of *John* xvi 32 καὶ οὐκ εἰμὶ μόνος ὅτι ὁ πατὴρ μετ' ἐμοῦ ἐστι. It is also possible that the Logion rests on Jewish traditional teaching; and in support of this Taylor[2] cites from the *Pirque Aboth* a saying of Rabbi Chalafta: 'When ten sit and are occupied in the words of Torah, the Shechina is among them...And whence (is it proved) of even three?...And whence even two?...And whence even one? Because it is said: "In all places where I record my name, I will come unto thee and I will bless thee."' But such an utterance lies nearer or perhaps is the germ of Matthew's saying concerning the two or three.

But if the canonical books can show no more than the elements out of which the Saying probably grew, uncanonical writers exhibit it fully formed and even advanced a stage. Clement of Alexandria[3] while defending marriage against the extreme ascetics has occasion to refer to the passage in *Matth.* xviii, interpreting the "Three" as husband, wife and child. A little later he writes: 'They (the ascetics) affirm that the Lord means that with the many (τῶν πλειόνων) is the Demiourgos, the productive god; but with the one—that is the elect—is the Saviour.' Later still[4], he tries another line of interpretation: 'perhaps with the One, the Jew, the Lord was in giving the Law; but in prophesying...he was gathering peoples...the Two; and a Third was being created out of the two unto a new man.' In the first of these passages we discern a Saying about One and οἱ πλείονες, and in the second about One, Two and Three; nor can we doubt that οἱ πλείονες of the first are equivalent to the Two and Three of the second passage. In a word, Clement's saying[5] went beyond the Logion in containing a clause about Three, and therefore cannot be identical with it. Such a three-clause Saying is actually preserved by Ephraem Syrus[6]: 'Ubi unus est, ibi et ego sum; et ubi duo sunt, ibi et ego ero; et quando tres sumus, quasi in ecclesia coimus.' It appears, therefore, that whereas the Logion in its revolt from the 'congregational condition' dropped the reference to the Three, the Saying which underlies Clement and that quoted by Ephraem (the two Sayings may or may not have been strictly identical), while starting with the Logion, went back to Matthew for this reference and so softened down the difference between the 'solitary' and the 'congregational' points of view.

---

[1] Cp. Badham *Athenaeum* Aug. 7, 1897 (reading, however, ὅπου εἰς ἐστιν, μόνος ζήτω).
[2] *Ox. Log.* p. 34.   [3] *Strom.* III 10 § 68.   [4] *Ib.* § 70.
[5] Robinson (*Expos.* 1897 p. 417) thinks Clement may be dealing with a Saying advanced by Cassianus from the *Gospel according to the Egyptians*: cf. Introd. p. xliii.
[6] Preuschen *Antilegomena* p. 31 no. 39.

On the other hand, the Logion is not to be taken as a recommendation of the solitary life, as Mr Badham[1] apparently regards it. If such were the meaning of the first part, it would surely have been developed in the second, which, in fact, refers to hard and common work. Moreover, this view does not assign its proper weight to the adverb[2]: the balancing of ὅπου...ὅπου in the first part against ἐκεῖ...ἐκεῖ in the second is surely not fortuitous, and the meaning must be not only 'When you are lonely, I am with you,' but 'Wherever you may be, and however lonely, I am there with you.' And lastly, if the Saying had been framed to console some 'ascetic of the Thebaid,' σχίσον τὸ ξύλον is very inappropriate: there is little wood in the retreats sought out by the solitaries of Upper Egypt.

In l. 24 the reading ἄθεοι, about which the discoverers[3] have some doubts, is established (as Harnack points out) by reference to Ephes. ii 12 μνημονεύετε...ὅτι ἦτε...χωρὶς Χριστοῦ...ἄθεοι ἐν τῷ κόσμῳ. This passage also exhibits the same Christology as the Logion, for in the one as in the other Χριστός is equated with θεός, a development which makes it impossible to regard the Saying as primary: the Synoptics do not positively record any claim of Christ to be identified with God.

The second part of the Saying presents little or no textual difficulty, but its interpretation has been much discussed. The chief lines of interpretation may be briefly summarised and discussed here.

(1) The raising of the stone

and the cleaving of the wood have been thought to carry a pantheistic meaning. Cersoy[4] thinks that divine immanence in matter (but not pantheism) is intended, and compares Psalms cxxxviii (cxxxix) 7 ff. Lock[5] believes likewise that the Logion asserts Christ's universal presence, but that it does not deny his personality by merging him in nature. In that case the articles are deictic and the first ἐκεῖ means 'in the wood'; but equally the second ἐκεῖ (after ἔγειρον τὸν λίθον) must mean 'under the stone'—a rendering which brings this line of interpretation to shipwreck[6]. Again, why 'raise the stone' but cleave the wood? Cersoy[7] again suggests that if the Saying can be assumed to be translated from Hebrew, 'raise' may be a mistake for 'hew,' since confusion between the two Hebrew words would be easy; but warrant would be needed for such an assumption. The discoverers aptly quoted the Saying from the Gospel of Eve: ἐγὼ σὺ καὶ σὺ ἐγώ· καὶ ὅπου ἐὰν ᾖς, ἐγὼ ἐκεῖ εἰμί, καὶ ἐν ἄπασίν εἰμι ἐσπαρμένος, καὶ ὅθεν ἐὰν θέλῃς συλλέγεις με, ἐμὲ δὲ συλλέγων ἑαυτὸν συλλέγεις, and though it is likely (as remarked above) that this is derived from the Logion or its source, the distance between the two is obvious. One of the critics has rightly remarked that later ages might easily read into this Logion a pantheistic meaning which was never intended: this seems to have been done by the formulator of the Saying in the Gospel of Eve.

(2) Dr Barnes finds an allegorical reference to the stone which

[1] Athen. Aug. 7, 1897.
[2] Cp. the fragment of the Gospel of Eve (Epiphanius Haer. XXVI 3) καὶ ὅπου ἐὰν ᾖς, ἐγὼ ἐκεῖ εἰμι, which would seem to be a recasting of this Logion.
[3] Λόγια Ἰησοῦ p. 13.
[4] Rev. Bibl. 1898 p. 419.   [5] Two Lectures pp. 24–5.
[6] See Taylor Ox. Log. p. 40.
[7] Op. cit. p. 420.

SAYINGS OF JESUS 39

closed the Sepulchre and to the wood of the cross, and this suggestion is commended by Lock[1], especially if the Logion can be supposed to be of comparatively late a date. There seems, however, to be a double objection to this view: first, everything goes to show that the 'Logia' (and the Sayings) are not of a late date[2]; and secondly it is hard to see why we are to cleave (not pierce) the wood of the cross: the cross does not hide anything. Dr Lock mentions another allegorical interpretation by which the stone becomes the stones of an altar, the wood, the wood of sacrifice, but objects that this would introduce a ritual long obsolete. More cogent still is the fact that so allegorized, the second part of the Saying altogether loses sight of the idea of loneliness dominant in the first part.

Professor Swete, again, believes this part of the Logion to start from *Eccles.* x 9 (quoted below), and that it refers to the building of the Church: *Matth.* xvi 18 might seem to give colour to this solution. Yet to accept it is to distort the parallelism with the result that loneliness is primarily emphasised in the first, and building in the second part.

(3) The discoverers with Dr James would lay stress on the imperatives, which indicate that strenuous effort is needed to realise the promise of the first half of the Saying; but here again the parallelism is disturbed in so far as 'effort' does not balance 'loneliness.'

(4) Harnack[3], like Swete, believes this half of the Saying to have started from *Eccles.* x 9

ἐξαίρων λίθους διαπονηθήσεται ἐν αὐτοῖς,

σχίζων ξύλα κινδυνεύσει ἐν αὐτοῖς,

and to be a conscious correction of its model: ἔγειρον should be read ἐξᾶρον[4]. Perhaps the correction is not needed; the compiler of the Saying need not be supposed to have turned to his text of *Ecclesiastes*, but probably relied on his memory and so wrote ἔγειρον instead of ἐξᾶρον. For the former word cf. *Matth.* xii 11. That ἔγειρον is the correct reading seems to be established by a citation, possibly from this very document or its source, in the *Etymolog. Gudianum,* ἔγειρε τὸν λίθον[5]: whether the Logion deliberately or unconsciously corrects the sentence of the Preacher must remain uncertain, but it is surely very difficult to resist Harnack's conclusion that the former is in some way dependent upon the latter. Possibly the connection is purely literary, and the compiler had no intent to correct his model. Harnack's presentation of the meaning of the Saying as a whole is admirable: 'The blessing' he writes[6] 'is not upon the work[7] [in itself]; yet the Saying is a protest against the idea that the presence of God is only to be obtained by fasting, prayer, and meditation....No, God is also present in the daily task, yet only if the disciple is really μόνος, *i.e.* separate from the world.' The

---

[1] *Two Lectures* p. 25.
[2] *Introduction* p. lxv.
[3] *Op. cit.* p. 19.
[4] Yet the discoverers retain their original reading, remarking that O is back-ligatured so that C rather than P would be expected, though bad writing may account for this (*Ox. Pap.* I p. 2). See also Wessely *Patr. Orient.* IV 155.
[5] See Reitzenstein *Ein Zitat aus den* Λόγια 'Ιησοῦ (*Zeitschr. f. neutest. Wissenschaft u. Kunde* VI (1905) p. 203).
[6] *Op. cit.* p. 21.
[7] Though the Saying preserved in Codex Bezae (Luke vi 4) [Preuschen *Antilegomena* p. 27 no. 8] might be taken as evidence to the contrary.

only objection to be raised is to the quasi-technical sense of μόνος, which leaves the reference to the Two who are not without God unexplained. Should we not rather take the protest to be directed against the idea that a formal congregation, as well as ceremonial procedure, is necessary to secure God's presence, and that common work is essentially non-religious, and paraphrase the Saying: 'No matter where or how lonely you may be—whether you are only two or even one; no matter that you are at your daily task, hard, common work;—God is present with you there[1]'? ἐκεῖ then (as its antithesis to ὅπου proves) means 'in the place where you are working.'

Lock finds difficulty alike in the singulars τὸν λίθον, τὸ ξύλον and in the aorists ἔγειρον (or ἐξᾶρον) and σχίσον, if such a line as Harnack has marked out is followed. But the language is surely semi-poetical, and the singular can be used legitimately just as we might say: 'Plough the field, turn the furrow'; and once the use of the singulars is admitted the aorists also are justified.

The second part of the Logion, or something like it, seems to have been known to the compiler of the extant recensions of the *Gospel according to Thomas*. Taylor has drawn attention to the passage εἶπε δὲ τῷ νεανίσκῳ· ἀνάστα νῦν, σχίζε τὰ ξύλα καὶ μνημόνευέ μου[2]. But if there is a real connection between the two it is obviously through one or more links which we can no longer recover. It may be worth while to remark on another passage[3] in the same Gospel where the injured builder is addressed : σοὶ λέγω ἄνθρωπε ἀνάστα ποίει τὸ ἔργον σου. The importance attached to work makes it possible that there is a remote connection with the Logion : and to a builder the words 'raise the stone, cleave the wood' would most appropriately be addressed. In view of the close connection between the Sayings and the Logia and the *Gospel according to the Hebrews*, "is it altogether fanciful to suggest that this Logion was addressed to that 'caementarius' with the withered hand of whom Jerome[4] has preserved notice?"

SAYING XI
[LOGION VI]

λέγει Ἰ(ησοῦ)ς·   30
οὐ|κ ἔστιν δεκτὸς προ-
φήτης ἐν τῇ π(ατ)ρίδι αὐ-
τ[ο]ῦ, οὐδὲ ἰατρὸς ποιεῖ
θεραπείας εἰς τοὺς
γεινώσκοντας αὐτό(ν).   35

---

[1] The condition "if you desire his presence" is of course understood : cf. *Apoc.* iii 20.
[2] A (ed. Tischendorf) x : cf. B ix.   [3] A xviii.
[4] *Comm. on Matth.* xii 13 [Preuschen *Antileg.* p. 5 no. 8].

Jesus saith :
A prophet is not acceptable in his own country,
Neither doth a physician do healing upon them who know him.

Each of the four Gospels has a parallel to the first part of this Logion. On the one hand we have *Mark* vi 4 οὐκ ἔστι προφήτης ἄτιμος εἰ μὴ ἐν τῇ πατρίδι αὐτοῦ καὶ ἐν τοῖς συγγενέσιν αὐτοῦ καὶ ἐν τῇ οἰκίᾳ αὐτοῦ, which is reproduced word for word (with the omission of καὶ ἐν τοῖς συγγενέσιν αὐτοῦ) in *Matth.* xiii 57, and is echoed more remotely in *John* iv 44 προφήτης ἐν τῇ ἰδίᾳ πατρίδι τιμὴν οὐκ ἔχει. On the other, Luke (iv 23–24) reproduces this Saying with characteristic editorial touches combined with other matter which is obviously related to the second part : πάντως ἐρεῖτέ μοι τὴν παραβολὴν ταύτην· Ἰατρέ, θεράπευσον σεαυτόν· ὅσα ἠκούσαμεν γενόμενα εἰς τὴν Καπερναούμ, ποίησον καὶ ὧδε ἐν τῇ πατρίδι σου. εἶπε δέ· ἀμὴν λέγω ὑμῖν ὅτι οὐδεὶς προφήτης δεκτός ἐστιν ἐν τῇ πατρίδι αὐτοῦ. On the purely verbal side, therefore, the Logion agrees with the Matthew-Mark version in reading οὐκ ἔστι προφήτης for the οὐδεὶς προφήτης of Luke. Yet this is so trifling and unimportant a point that it is quite impossible to claim it as indicating the influence either of Matthew or of Mark. The same cannot be said of the use of δεκτός, which is Lucan, in place of the ἄτιμος of Matthew and Mark. It is a literary improvement such as is characteristic of Luke, and was probably suggested to him by the citation from *Isaiah* lxi in *v.* 19 (κηρῦξαι ἐνιαυτὸν Κυρίου δεκτόν). The whole Lucan account of the visit to Nazareth is extremely interesting as throwing light on the evangelist's literary methods. Luke has made the visit to Nazareth the

first incident after the Temptation —an order which (if we are to accept the earlier Marcan arrangement) is artificial and unhistorical. Clearly Luke felt a literary and dramatic necessity to make Nazareth the scene of the first public appearance of Jesus, and has rearranged his material accordingly[1]. Luke, indeed, betrays himself by referring in iv 23 to mighty works done in Capernaum which he actually records under the ensuing visit to that town (iv 31 ff.). Not only is the position of the Nazareth incident unhistorical, but the discourse in the Synagogue in all probability is also. Dr Swete[2] indeed thinks that ' Luke described the scene from the recollections of some eyewitness, perhaps the Mother of the Lord.' But since the manipulation of the incident to make it a dramatic opening of a prophet's career is purely unhistorical, the references to the prophets Elijah and Elishah (*vv.* 25 ff.) are equally so : their purpose is to emphasize the compiler's view of the episode. This being so, it is almost certain that all the non-Marcan portion of the Lucan passage was evolved by the evangelist from his own feeling of what the situation (as arranged by him) required. Accordingly, he begins with the reading from *Isaiah* of the passage most appropriate to the opening of the ministry, followed by the direct claim to prophetic functions, 'Today is this scripture fulfilled in your ears.' Then, reverting to his source, he represents the people of Nazareth as scornful of Jesus because they know his origin, and

[1] Cf. Holtzmann *Life of Jesus* (E.T.) pp. 276–7.
[2] *Gospel acc. to St Mark* p. 111.

42 SAYINGS OF JESUS

finding in his source (*Mark* vi 5) the notice 'he could do there no mighty work, save that he laid his hands upon a few sick folk and healed them,' saw his way to quote the proverb 'Physician, heal thyself' as part of the assumed jeers of the men of Nazareth. Next follows the Saying concerning the fate of a prophet in his own country, somewhat awkwardly inset by aid of the repeated εἶπε δέ. And lastly, the assumed challenge of the men of Nazareth to Jesus to do mighty works in his own country as he had done in Capernaum, is met by the declaration that as Elijah and Elishah were forced to limit their miraculous powers, so also the prophet, who had lately arisen amongst them, would do. This digression may be summed up in a sentence: the character of the discourse in the Synagogue is such as to prove it subsidiary to Luke's purpose in moving forward the visit to Nazareth and making it the significant opening episode of the prophetic ministry of Jesus, and the whole incident (excepting such parts as are guaranteed by Mark) is purely Lucan in origin.

δεκτός in the Logion, therefore, is directly borrowed from Luke, and the same must be true of the second part of the Logion since it is made up of purely Lucan materials. This part shows exactly the same method of composition as do Sayings III and IV, which consists in choosing a Saying from one of the Gospels already existing as a nucleus and expanding and developing this either for literary purposes or to include fresh phases of thought. In the present case the compiler seems to have aimed

partly at the formation of a parallelism, and partly at the contrivance of an apt retort to the proverb 'Physician, heal thyself'[1] —a retort which underlies the reference to the examples of Elijah and Elishah. The force of the Saying as a whole may perhaps be brought out by paraphrasing:— 'You scorn me as a prophet because you know whence I am and challenge me to work miracles amongst my own people as I have done amongst strangers: I reply that as you reject the spiritual blessings I offer, you shall not share in the temporal blessings I would otherwise bestow.'

Swete remarks that the second part of the Logion is not, in its literal sense, true, and thinks that the physician must be a physician of the soul. But to accept this view would be to ignore the literal sense of the Lucan parallel; and in a retort such as this some latitude for inexactness must be allowed. I am not sure, also, that the two clauses are not intended as protasis and apodosis of a conditional sentence: 'If the prophet is not accepted by his own people, then the physician will not heal his own kin.'

The Saying shows traces which indicate either an Aramaic original or a compiler whose native tongue was Aramaic. In ll. 33–34 the phrase ποιεῖ θεραπείας is considered by Cersoy to betray an Aramaic original; but, as Taylor notes, the phrase is also found in the *Protevangelium Jacobi* (XX). In l. 35 γεινώσκοντας αὐτόν answers generally to ⟨τοῖς συγγενέσιν⟩ καὶ ἐν τῇ οἰκίᾳ of Mark and Matthew: Swete[2] compares *Psalms* lxxxvi (lxxxvii) 4 τοῖς γινώσκουσί με,

---

[1] In the Introduction (p. xxxvi) I have shown reason for believing that the Sayings were extracts: in the present case the Saying of Jesus was no doubt preceded by the physician-proverb which was put directly (not indirectly as Luke has it) into the mouths of the people of Nazareth.

[2] *Expository Times* Sept. 1897 p. 548.

and suggests an Aramaic source. Cersoy suggests that there may be a mistranslation here where εἰς τοὺς γνωστοὺς αὐτοῦ is required.

Such a slip might have occurred in translation from either an Aramaic or a Hebrew document.

SAYING XII

[Logion VII]

λέγει Ἰ(ησοῦ)ς·
πόλις ᾠκοδο-
μημένη ἐπ' ἄκρον
[ὄ]ρους ὑψηλοῦ καὶ ἐσ-
τηριγμένη οὔτε πε-
[σ]εῖν δύναται οὔτε κρυ-   40
[β]ῆναι.

36. ΟΙΚΟΔΟΜΗΜΕΝΗ, *P*, corr. by *GH*.   38. ΥΨΗΛΟΥC, *P*, corr. by the original hand.

Jesus saith:
A city built upon the top of a high mountain and established
Can neither fall nor be hidden.

Batiffol[1] considers that the Saying has lost its true parallelistic form, for (as Harnack remarks) the fall of a whole city would be quite extraordinary whereas a single house might easily fall, and a part of the Logion is, in fact, dependent upon the Parable of the House upon the Sands. The original form would then be: 'A city built upon the top of a mountain cannot be hid, And a house established upon a high rock (or hill) cannot fall.' This has the advantage of restoring true parallelism and is probably correct. We may cite in support of this correction *Isaiah* ii 2 ὅτι ἔσται ἐν ταῖς ἐσχάταις ἡμέραις ἐμφανὲς τὸ ὄρος κυρίου καὶ ὁ οἶκος τοῦ θεοῦ ἐπ' ἄκρου τῶν ὀρέων[2], a passage which probably

suggested to the compiler the idea of conflating the two New Testament Sayings (see below). Probably the confusion resulted in translation from an Aramaic original in which the word for 'house' had dropped out, causing a difficulty which the translator met in representing the city as unable either to fall or to be hid: he would seem to have manufactured a forced parallelism in which ᾠκοδο-μημένη and ἐστηριγμένη are intended to balance οὔτε πεσεῖν and οὔτε κρυβῆναι. In support of the opposite view that the Saying is in its original form, we may argue that the compiler was so bent on combining the two ideas of conspicuousness and stability that he overlooked the objection that a

[1] *Rev. Bibl.* 1897 p. 511.   [2] Cp. *Micah* iv 1

city as a whole does not fall (thus in *Apoc.* xi 13 only a tenth part of the city falls as the result of 'a great earthquake'), and that the correction separates ὑψηλοῦ from ὅρους, while the actual reading has the support of *Isaiah* xxviii 4 καὶ ἔσται τὸ ἄνθος τὸ ἐκπεσὸν τῆς ἐλπίδος τῆς δόξης ἐπ᾽ ἄκρου τοῦ ὅρους τοῦ ὑψηλοῦ. On the whole, however, the arguments in favour of Batiffol's change seem to have more weight.

The first part of the Logion depends upon Matthew alone : οὐ δύναται πόλις κρυβῆναι ἐπάνω ὅρους κειμένη (v 14). The variant ἐπ᾽ ἄκρον τοῦ ὅρους for Matthew's ἐπάνω is probably due to the influence of *Isaiah* ii 2, quoted above (or even of *Isaiah* xxviii 4 ; but the phrase is common in the Old Testament). ᾠκοδομημένη, as Lock points out[1], is decidedly interesting as it is indicated as a variant for Matthew's κειμένη by the early Syriac versions, by Tatian, by one Latin version, and by a passage from the *Clementine Homilies* (III 67) quoted by Har-

nack : χρὴ οὖν τὴν ἐκκλησίαν ὡς πόλιν ἐν ὕψει ᾠκοδομημένην φιλόθεον ἔχειν τάξιν καὶ διοίκησιν καλήν.

This last passage together with *Isaiah* ii 2 is evidence enough to show that both 'house' and 'city' signify the Christian Church—an idea which is not unsynoptic :. cf. *Matth.* v 14; xvi 18.

The second part of the Logion is parallel to the Parable of the Wise and Foolish Housebuilders (*Matth.* vii 24–25 = *Luke* vi 47–49), and the verbal resemblance of the Logion to *Matthew* is so close that to deny direct dependence is difficult indeed : the words ᾠκοδομημένη...ἐστηριγμένη...οὔτε πεσεῖν of the former being echoes of Matthew's ᾠκοδόμησε ... τεθεμελίωτο ἐπὶ τὴν πέτραν (ἐστηριγμένη is a convenient abbreviation)...οὐκ ἔπεσεν. Luke, it must be noticed, shows no such verbal parallels.

In this Logion, therefore, we have a clear instance of conflation, a process which we have seen to be characteristic of the *Gospel according to the Hebrews* (Introduction p. lxii).

SAYING XIII

[LOGION VIII]

λέγει Ἰ(ησοῦ)ς·

ἀκούεις

[ε]ἰς τὸ ἓ[ν ὠ]τίον σου, τὸ

[δὲ ἕτερον συνέκλεισας].

42. [.]ιϲ το ε..τιον ϲου τω, *P* : εἰς τὸ ἐνώπιον, *GH* : εἰς τὸ ἐνώτιον (εἰς τὸ ἐν ὠτίον, *Taylor*) σου, τὸ δὲ ἕτερον συνέκλεισας, *Swete* : ἀκούεις εἰς τὸ ἐν ὠτίον σου, τὸ δὲ ἕτερον ἔβυσας, *Lock, Sanday* : τῷ δὲ ἑτέρῳ παρακούεις, *Sanday* : ⟨ἃ⟩ ἀκούεις, εἰς τὸ ἐν ὠτίον σου τὸ δεξιόν, *Zahn* : ἄκουε ἴσως εἰς τὸ ἐναντίον σου στόμα[2], *Bruston* : εἰς τὸ ταμεῖόν σου, *Badham*.

---

[1] *Two Lectures* pp. 13 and 26.   [2] Cf. also *Paroles de Jésus* p. 10.

Jesus saith :
Thou hearest with one ear,
But the other hast thou closed.

The restorations of Swete, Taylor, Lock and Sanday follow one general type and have the same general sense. Bruston, following Batiffol's hint[1], would make this the commencement of the first Logion: this view has been discussed and rejected in the commentary on that Saying. Zahn's suggestion, 'What thou hearest, (hear) with thy right ear alone...' is ingenious and has the support of the passages collected by Dr Taylor[2] to show the importance attached by the -Jews to the right ear. It is, however, too ingenious, and the English type of restoration is far more simple, natural and direct. I have preferred Swete's conjecture (with Taylor's division ἐν ὠτίον).

The discoverers, followed apparently by most editors, take the meaning to be 'Thou imperfectly understandest my message.' This does not seem quite adequate. Is there not an implication of wilful deafness in τὸ δὲ ἕτερον συνέκλεισας which is more fully brought out by rendering 'You listen to me so far as outward hearing goes, but have closed the ears of your spiritual hearing against conviction[3]'? The Logion is, in fact, a masterly analysis of the attitude of those who instinctively close their hearts to unwelcome truth: compare generally *Matth.* xiii 13 ἀκούοντες ἀκούουσι οὐδὲ συνιοῦσι, which is proved by vv. 14-15 to refer to wilful hardness and not to natural weakness of comprehension; and *Luke* vi 46, 'Why call ye me Lord, Lord, and do not the things which I say[4]?'

The use of the second person singular makes it most likely that the Saying was addressed to an individual—as to the rich young ruler of *Matth.* xix 16-22, *Luke* xviii 23. It is noteworthy that this incident recurred in the *Gospel according to the Hebrews*[5].

---

[1] *Rev. Bibl.* 1897 p. 511 n. 1.   [2] *Ox. Log.* pp. 63-5.
[3] Somewhat similar is Scott's Introduction to *Old Mortality*: 'Old Mortality was not one of those religious devotees, who, although one eye is seemingly turned towards heaven, keep the other steadfastly fixed on some sublunary object.'
[4] Compare further *Luke* viii 14 οὗτοί εἰσιν οἱ ἀκούσαντες, καὶ ὑπὸ μεριμνῶν καὶ πλούτου καὶ ἡδονῶν τοῦ βίου...συμπνίγονται.
[5] Preuschen *Antilegomena* p. 6 no. 11.

INDEX

[NOTE. Only the more important names and topics discussed are included in this Index. References to the names of scholars and editors are given where the view expressed is of special importance.]

For EU product safety concerns, contact us at Calle de José Abascal, 56–1°, 28003 Madrid, Spain or eugpsr@cambridge.org.

www.ingramcontent.com/pod-product-compliance
Ingram Content Group UK Ltd.
Pitfield, Milton Keynes, MK11 3LW, UK
UKHW020313140625
459647UK00018B/1852